A PEOPLE AND THEIR QUILTS

In the late afternoon, the Tyler Bunches sun their quilts and themselves at their home in Hancock County, Tennessee.

A PEOPLE AND THEIR

QUILTS

by John Rice Irwin

Schiffer Publishing Ltd

4880 Lower Valley Road, Atglen, PA 19310 USA

Dedication

Dedicated to the pioneer women of America and their daughters, who spent untold hours creating one of the most useful and most beautiful objects of our culture; and who are only now beginning to receive deserved recognition for their prodigious toil and artistic talent.

Published by Schiffer Publishing Ltd.
4880 Lower Valley Road
Atglen, PA 19310
Phone: (610) 593-1777; Fax: (610) 593-2002
E-mail: Schifferbk@aol.com
Please visit our web site catalog at **www.schifferbooks.com**

In Europe, Schiffer books are distributed by Bushwood Books
6 Marksbury Avenue Kew Gardens
Surrey TW9 4JF England
Phone: 44 (0) 20-8392-8585; Fax: 44 (0) 20-8392-9876
E-mail: Bushwd@aol.com
Free postage in the UK. Europe: air mail at cost.

This book may be purchased from the publisher.
Include $3.95 for shipping. Please try your bookstore first.
We are always looking for people to write books on new and related subjects.
If you have an idea for a book please contact us at the above address.
You may write for a free catalog.

Other Books by John Rice Irwin

Marcellus Moss Rice and His Big Valley Kinsmen
Musical Instruments of the Southern Appalachian Mountains
Guns and Gunmaking Tools of Southern Appalachia
The Arnwine Cabin
Baskets and Basket Makers in Southern Appalachia
Alex Stewart, Portrait of a Pioneer

Unless otherwise noted, the photographs were taken by Robin Hood.

Copyright © 1984 by John Rice Irwin.
Library of Congress Catalogue Number 83-61649.

ISBN: 0-88740-024-8
Printed in China.

Acknowledgments

The author wishes to publicly express his gratitude to all those who willingly shared their quilts, expertise, and time in connection with the writing of this book. First, my friend Robin Hood's contribution to this endeavor is evident on nearly every page. Not only are his photographs truly superb, but he has been a most dedicated and cooperative co-worker as well, traveling the back roads and mountains for what often proved to be long and tiring hours. One evening we arrived at my home after midnight following twenty hours of non-stop traveling, interviewing, and photographing. I left him in the den talking on the phone with his wife Peggy. When I arose the next morning he was still sitting by the phone where he had spent the night, too tired to walk to the bedroom. After breakfast and a few cups of coffee he was ready for another day.

I must not forget Pat Hudson, reference librarian and free lance writer from Knoxville, who has done a masterful job in translating my conglomeration of words into something approaching the English language. Janice Stokes, likewise, is to be most highly commended for her ability to read, decipher, and type my longhand, or more aptly my version of shorthand. Judy Elwood has been an able advisor in helping to identify quilt patterns, and offering advice based on her practical knowledge and professional expertise as a quilter. My friend Jess Butcher, who is personally acquainted with thousands of folks from presidents to mountain hermits, has helped me track down a number of old time quilters. And to Andrea Fritts and my wife Elizabeth I should offer thanks for helping with the Museum and for manning the telephones during my preoccupation with this project.

There are dozens of other people whose assistance has been of great value. A partial listing of these unselfish contributors would be worse than no list at all. Hence, no effort will be made here to identify each of the several dozen people who have assisted in various ways in the compilation of this work. Many are mentioned in the body of the book, and to those not mentioned it is hoped that the results of their assistance are reflected in the book to their satisfaction.

The Pineapple motif, found in varied forms, dates to the 1700's. This one was made in Sevier County, Tennessee, and now belongs to Catherine Arnold of California. It is sometimes called Pineapple Log Cabin. (Photographed at the Museum of Appalachia)

Table of Contents

Introduction

"I'd druther quilt than to eat on the hungriest day that ever I seen."

-Ethel Hall, Viper, Kentucky

Tyler Bunch, one of several men quilters included in the book, is shown here being interviewed by the author.

Few items in our culture have been so necessary, colorful, artistic, cherished, cared for, and universally used as the quilt. In over a quarter century of collecting relics throughout the Southern Appalachian mountains for the Museum of Appalachia in Norris, Tennessee, I have had occasion to go through literally thousands of homes — from the smallest one-room mountain cabin, to the palatial antebellum homes along the riverways. I recall only a single instance where the chattels of a household did not include quilts.

The quilt, perhaps as much as any household item, tended to be made by the family which used it. Probably no craft (or art form) was more widely practiced by women in all stations of life than quilting — not only in this country but in the lands from whence the early settlers came. From Mary Stuart, Queen of Scots, to maidens in the most impoverished European cottages, and in America from wives of Presidents to women living in one-room, dirt-floored frontier cabins, the needles flew, and beautiful as well as useful quilts were made.

Several books have been written on the subject of quilts in America, usually emphasizing the inestimable variety of patterns, the artistic qualities, and the intricate and detailed stitching. Many of these works place heavy emphasis upon the technical aspects of specific patterns, and several are "how to" books. The area which seems to have been neglected is that which deals with quilts in direct relation to *people*. Coincidentally, this is an area where my greatest interest lies. Hence this book deals with quilts as they relate to the people who made, used, and enjoyed them. Emphasis is placed on quilts and quilters in the states located within the Southern Appalachian region, with comparisons and contrasts to quilts and quilters in various part of America and other countries which influenced our quilt-making culture.

It would be wonderful if we could view the old time quilt makers as they plied their craft and attended quilting bees so that we could learn firsthand the lore of one of our country's most prevalent and most beloved art and craft forms. But this scene has largely passed in most areas, except for the revivalist — the younger folk who have taken up their grandmother's ways.

One of the areas in America where old time quilting never altogether ceased was Southern Appalachia. This is a suitable area to study the American quilt because the region was settled by diversified groups including the Pennsylvania Dutch, the Welsh, the English, the Scotch-Irish, the blacks and the French-Huguenots, and because those who immigrated from this region, after a generation or two, helped to populate a large part of the United States; the Midwest first, then Texas, the far West and the Northwest. Therefore, kinship exists between the Southern Appalachian region and other areas of the country.

With few exceptions, each type of quilt found in the rest of the country may be found in this area. Because of economic and geographic conditions in the region, quilting flourished longer here than anywhere else. In fact, it never really ceased being popular among the women of this area. While store-bought blankets became popular in other sections of the country, the quilt remained the mainstay in Appalachia. When the quilt revival began sweeping the country, the art-craft had to be resurrected in most areas, but it had never died here.

This region provides a glimpse into a lifestyle related to quilts that no longer exists in more urbanized, industralized and less isolated regions. A look at these folk may provide a semblance of what quilters and quilting were like throughout the country in the early days. The photographs, interviews, and conversations included in the following chapters are provided as steps for more serious and competent researchers who may follow.

ROSE OF SHARON
(Pennsylvania Bridal Quilt)

In the village of New Alexandria, a few miles east of Pittsburg, Pennsylvania, Anna Reed made this beautiful Rose of Sharon as a bridal quilt probably for her own trousseau. Anna was born in 1831 and the quilt is believed to have been made about 1850.

Anna Reed never had use for the bridal quilt, for she never married. In later years, she gave it to her niece, Bella Reed, who passed it on to her nephew William Reed and his wife Mary McNaughton Reed who, since 1937, have made their home in Toledo, Ohio.

This appliqued quilt was never used before it came into the possession of the Reeds, and then only sparingly, and was probably washed only once in its one hundred thirty years. At the urging of her daughter, Judy Krupp of Kingston, Tennessee, Mary Reed entered this quilt in the Museum of Appalachia's 1983 Spring Quilt Show and won first place in Best Antique Quilt category.

Chapter I

The Quilt Comes to America

CAKESTAND AND CONTRARY WIFE

Quilt pattern names frequently relate to pioneer times, historic events, political figures, or foreign countries. The pattern names do not often relate to household items or to women themselves. These two quilts are exceptions.

The Cakestand quilt, at left, was purchased at public auction from the McCloud estate sale at Halls Cross Roads, Knox County, Tennessee. The McClouds reportedly settled there soon after the American Revolution. The road on

which the homeplace was located is named Tom McCloud Road after the man of that name who was known as "Buttermilk" Tom because he peddled buttermilk in the nearby city of Knoxville. The quilt is pieced and has intricate stitching.

The Contrary Wife quilt, on the right, is also from Knox County, Tennessee. It has a wide, blue border set back from the edge, and the colors are patriotic red, white and blue.

Grandfather Irwin often told the story of a poor young lad named Calloway McGhee who would come to his father's home in the dead of winter, barefoot and coatless, to get some corn or a few potatoes for his destitute family. "I've seen him a many a time come hopping through the snow with no shoes on, and him about froze to death. There was fourteen children in our family and we had to be mighty saving," Grandpa said. "But Mama would always give that poor boy something to eat, and sometimes an old coat. Well, in a few days he'd be back, and he wouldn't have his coat on. Mama 'ud say, 'Calloway, what happened to yer coat?' And he'd say, 'Mama cut it up to make a quilt.'" Grandpa would chuckle at the recollection of poor Calloway, and then he'd repeat his answer: "Mama cut it up to make a quilt."

This is illustrative of the importance attached to the quilt in frontier-type conditions in this country. That a mother would use her son's only coat to make a quilt is undisputed proof of the value placed on having adequate bed covers.

In 1962, as Superintendent of Schools in Anderson County, Tennessee, I visited a home in a remote section of the Cumberland mountains to determine why none of the thirteen children were attending school. My attendance teacher told me that many children were missing school because of a lack of clothing, and I wanted a firsthand look.

The house consisted of only two ordinary sized rooms, and both were all but void of furniture. One room served as a kitchen, but it had only a tiny laundry-type stove, a small table, a crude plank bench, and two or three chairs. The other room had two beds, a threadbare couch, and no heat. There was, of course no inside plumbing, and I never knew how far they had to carry their water.

The house was dark, lighted only by one curtainless window. At first I didn't notice the contents of the big bed in the corner of the room, but as my eyes adjusted to the dim light, there slowly appeared the forms of six small bodies in the bed with only their heads peering from the heavy quilts. They were wide awake, perfectly still, and deathly quiet.

My assumption that they were sick was quickly dispelled when their mother told me that they were in bed to keep warm. "We ain't got no heat, an' none of 'em have enough clothes to keep 'em warm; so hit's jest keep 'em in bed 'er let 'em freeze. If it wasn't fer the bed kivers I guess we'd all freeze."

I never pass that little shotgun cabin hanging on the side of a steep bank, without thinking of those children, lying there in the late afternoon, peering wide-eyed and silent from under the big patchwork quilt. And the quilt was the only colorful object in the otherwise drab and austere little house. Twenty years later, in 1982, several of these same children visited me and I was amazed at how healthy and prosperous they appeared to be. One was a postal employee in Birmingham, one was a school teacher in Ohio, and all the others had respectable jobs and seemed to be well-adjusted, middle-class citizens.

The process of quilting, in the most general sense, is the joining together of two pieces of material and a central filling by stitching the three layers together. Although the stitching originated for the practical purpose of holding the filling in place, the intricacy and minuteness of this stitching soon became as much aesthetic as utilitarian.

The word quilt is of Latin derivation, believed to have come from the word "Culcita" which means "stuffed sock, mattress or cushion." While the above definition is generally accepted it is not broad enough to embrace all items we refer to as quilts. For example, the top and back are sometimes "quilted," or sewn together without a padding and this is called a quilt. Sometimes two pieces of material, and the stuffing, are secured together by "tacking" or "tying," a process discussed in connection with comforters in Chapter IV, and this too is called a quilt. Although we generally refer to these two types as quilts, neither of them fits the definition as given.

In many parts of rural America, bed covers (or bed kivers) have been synonymous with quilts, but quilted material for clothing and even carpets seems to have been the oldest and most popular form. Documentation of quilted clothing goes back as far as 3000 B.C. The art-craft of quilting was practiced by the ancient Chinese, Egyptians, Greeks, and by virtually all civilizations, as cloth was developed.

It has been documented that many warriors who participated in the Crusades, starting in the 12th century, used quilted padding beneath their armour. Some suggest that these Crusaders, who marched from the Western European countries to crush the Moslems in the Holy Land, first became acquainted with quilted material in the Middle East and carried it back to their households.

Great catastrophies sometimes have beneficial by-products, and the popularization of the quilt is said to have been largely brought about by such a calamity. In Europe in the 14th century, severely cold weather which came to be known as the Great Freeze lasted for a number of winters, and caused the major rivers such as the Thames, the Rhine, and the Rhone to freeze solidly. Partly for necessity, and partly to relieve themselves from the boredom resulting from prolonged confinement, women busied themselves with making quilted material for garments and bed coverings.

The first quilts may have been purely for utilitarian use, but it wasn't long before decorative and artistic qualities were added. The French are largely credited with introducing floral applique. Quilting in Italy was centered mainly in Sicily and stressed aesthetics rather than warmth and comfort.

Quilting in England became widespread as early as the fifteenth century. In the British Isles and Low Countries, quilting became a cottage industry where women made quilts for their own use and to sell or trade for other commodities. Prior to the Industrial Revolution in the late 1700's, cloth was heavy, home-spun and home-woven. This hand-woven cloth continued to be used for making quilts in America in isolated areas for another hundred years.

Elizabeth Smith Schabel, in an article published in the *Tennessee Folklore Society Bulletin* (1981) writes that there are no records to indicate that early colonists brought quilts with them to America. She found no reference to quilts in America until the latter part of the seventeenth century, a half century after the first settlers arrived. Other students of the subject feel quilts were surely among the possessions brought to the New World by the early colonists, but that they failed to survive because of the limited life of textiles generally, and because of their continuous use.

Patsy and Myron Orlofsky, in their well researched and documented book *Quilts in America,* make reference to a calico quilt, "Colored and flowered" listed in the inventory of Captain George Corwin who died in Salem, Massachusetts in 1685. The Orlofsky's also note that a list of Captain John Kidd's chattels, when he and his wife Sarah started housekeeping in New York in 1692, included featherbeds, feather pillows, tablecloths, linen sheets, napkins, ten blankets and three quilts. (This is the same Captain Kidd who later gained infamy as a pirate.) There is little doubt that quilts have been an integral part of American households since the country's earliest days.

America is credited with the development of the rifled gun (the Kentucky rifle), which revolutionized weaponry; but the rifling of gun barrels had been experimented with in Germany long before. The dulcimer is called an American instrument, yet its "ancestors" were developed in mainland Europe. Likewise, the patchwork quilt is said by many to be an American innovation, yet it developed from antecedents in the old countries. Just as the rifle and the dulcimer have antecedents in Europe, the Kentucky Rifle and the mountain dulcimer have distinctly American forms, as does the patchwork quilt. The patchwork and other types, are discussed more thoroughly in Chapter IV.

Quilting bees, or quilting parties, even more than patchwork quilts, are sometimes considered an American innovation. Frontier conditions necessitated almost constant work, leaving little time for pleasure. Strict religious beliefs often discouraged social or recreational gatherings. But quilting bees, while often characterized as joyful occasions, could be justified because they were ostensibly for the purposes of accomplishment — at least enough so to satisfy the protestant work ethic.

Amanda McDowell, as a young lady writing in her diary in 1863 in White County, Tennessee, raised this interesting question. Should she join in a quilting held on Christmas Day? The question is especially meaningful when one considers that this was in the midst of the Civil War and that most of the boys her age, including some of her brothers, were fighting and dying on both sides of the struggle. Her answer seems to be that she personally saw nothing wrong with such an event, but that she would not sponsor it because of what others would think and say. The diary entry is as follows:

December 24, 1863

Christmas Eve. I have been baking some just for old custom's sake. For I do not look for anyone. But perhaps Fayette will come in a few days, though I hear they are gone to Kentucky. I feel lonely, but that is nothing uncommon. If there is any gayety about, I do not know where it is. Though I hear of a quilting tomorrow. I would not make a quilting on that day, (Christmas) but if I wanted one would make it sometime during the holidays, but it seems a little like profanation. Though I suppose it is no harm to be joyful on that day, but how many are there who think of the thing that ought to cause it to be a day of rejoicing and thanksgiving?

If the women weren't allowed, by husbands or fathers or their own conscience to participate in social gatherings as such, they could hardly be scolded for getting together for such a necessary and worthwhile purpose as quilting. It is not clear how often social events such as quilting bees occurred.

There seems to be no doubt that numerous chores in frontier society were accomplished, at least on occasion, by "workings," or group participation. Historian Dr. J. G. M. Ramsey lived during the frontier period and alluded to the quilting bee as an integral part of the social life of that period. He wrote:

> A failure to ask a neighbour to a raising, a clearing, a chopping frolic, or his family to a quilting, was considered a high indignity; such a one, too, as required to be explained or atoned for at the next muster or county court. Each settler was not only willing, but desirous to contribute his share to the general comfort and public improvement, and felt aggrieved and insulted if the opportunity to do so were withheld. (*The Annals of Tennessee*)

Women attended quilting bees and quilting parties while none of the other household chores warranted such gatherings. Baking, making kraut, drying fruit, or butchering animals was not an occasion for such "parties." Quilting bees often involved a community endeavor to make a present for one of its members. The church members made quilts for their preacher. Quilts were made for a young lady of the community as a wedding present, and the girls and young women made quilts for the young men of their community. These were sometimes signed by the girls and were known as Friendship quilts. Many quilting bees were held to make a quilt for the family in whose home it was "set up." Diaries, letters and other documents report a woman "putting up a quilt" and then inviting her neighbors. She would "put out the word" or actually send some member of the family (usually a young boy) around the community to announce the event. One might think this practice would have been viewed as a means of soliciting free labor. However, as Ramsey pointed out, indignation most

TWO EAST TENNESSEE QUILTS

These are representative of the beautiful and finely made quilts made during the final two or three decades of the last century. The one at left, The Rocky Road to Kansas, is from Blount County, in the extreme eastern part of Tennessee. It has a walnut dyed lining and is pieced from scrap material.

The quilt lying on the back of the wagon is similar to Odd Fellow's Cross, and was made in Hancock County, Tennessee. Although this is a remote and mountainous county (considered by the United States Government to be the third poorest in the entire nation) the people of this area have produced some of the finest country antiques found in Southern Appalachia. This pieced quilt has floral designed quilting.

frequently resulted, not from *being* invited to help one's neighbor at such affairs, but from *not* being invited.

A number of women interviewed about quilting bees knew grandmothers whose memories went back as far as the pioneer period. Most of the women never participated in any kind of gathering for the purposes of quilting except in the 1920's and 1930's, when quilting was enjoying a healthy revival. Little evidence exists to indicate that quilting parties were a universal practice in the pioneer-frontier era.

I asked Clemmie Pugh, who was 100 years old at the time, if she attended or knew about quilting parties. She was a girl in the mountains of Overton County, Tennessee in the 1880's and 1890's. "No. Didn't have nothing in our country like that. Everybody was poor, and we didn't ever have any get-togethers in the country — no way to go anyplace."

Tiny Baker was 92 years of age when she was asked about quilting bees. She was living in rural Knox County, Tennessee, in a log house where she was born. Her father, preacher Tom Baker, and

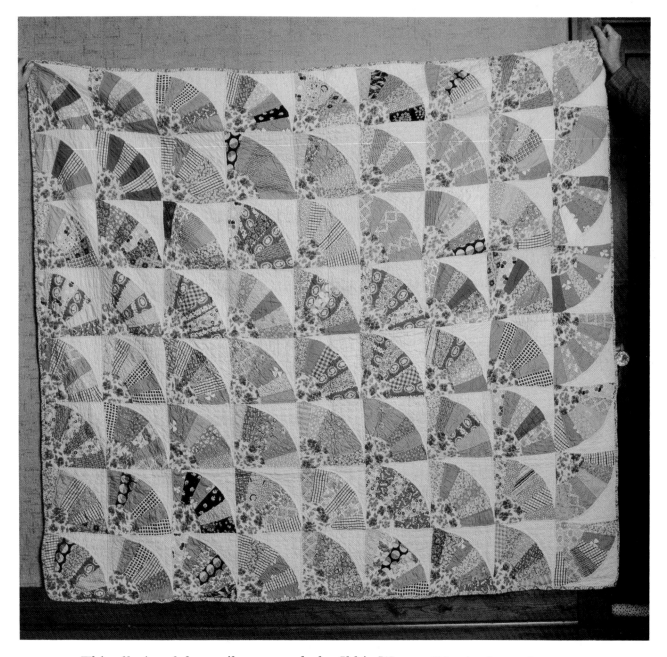

This all pieced fan quilt was made by Ibbie Weaver Rice in the early 1900's.

his father, Anderson Baker, were also born in this same house built by the family in the early 1830's. Tiny was most knowledgeable about the past, but she did not recall much about the quilting bee. "Oh, I've heard of quilting bees, but none of our folks, that I know of, ever was involved in sich as that. Now, there'd be several women who was members of the family that would get together and quilt, but as far as just getting up and going to a quilting party, I don't remember any of the old folks ever doing that."

Jettie Smith does remember what she calls quilting parties when she was a girl growing up in Poor Land Valley, in the rural East Tennessee County of Union during World War I. "Well, somebody would put out the word that they's having a quilting party on a certain night, and several of the neighborhood women would gather in. They'd either walk or ride a mule; but of course most of them lived fairly close. They wouldn't come from too far away."

I asked her if the men usually attended. "No, jest the women. They'd generally have popcorn, baked sweet potatoes and molasses candy to eat, and they'd all set around and quilt 'til bed time."

Opal Hatmaker (who is discussed extensively in chapter VI) grew up in the same period in a coal mining area near Briceville, some thirty miles west of Knoxville. My questions regarding the quilting bee evoked fond memories for her.

"Oh, yes, I had a many a quilting bee. If I wanted to have a quilting, I'd put the word out, usually at the church that I had a quilt up, and that we's having a quilting."

There is no doubt that the quilting bee was more common in some sections of the country than in others. Such events may have been more common in the more well-to-do areas, and were not as common in the frontier era as we may have been led to believe. Stephen Foster's *"Seeing Nellie Home"* and his allusion to *"Aunt Dinah's quilting party"* may have contributed to that exaggerated notion. Most of the early homes consisted of one or two rooms, and the families were large. Hence, the lack of space itself would have been a deterrent. The fact that women, as a rule, had several children to care for made it even more difficult. Evidence suggests that most quilts were not made at "quilting bees," and the quilting party was not commonplace in all areas and in all eras of American history.

Misleading general statements about quilts also have been made regarding geographical origins. For example, that the quilts of the South were more ornate, colorful, and artistic because there was more leisure among the ladies of that area. This may have been true in the homes of a small minority of affluent plantation homes in some sections of some states in the South. However, a statement of this sort is like saying all Japanese make silk, everybody in West Virginia mines coal, or that all Californians are movie stars. If a general statement could be made about the quilters of the "South" I should think the opposite would more likely be true. Nevertheless, there were many similarities in the development of quilts in America. Types of quilt patterns and their names are remarkably similar throughout the country.

Oscar Blevins is shown at the Blevins homestead built by his ancestors near the Big South Fork River in Scott County, Tennessee. The quilt shown on page 18 was found in this log cabin and acquired from Oscar, the last family member to live here. (Photograph taken in 1982 by Gary Hamilton)

BLEVINS FAMILY FRONTIER QUILT

The Blevins were among the first hunters to penetrate the wilderness area of Kentucky and the northern borders of Tennessee in the Cumberland Mountain area. When Daniel Boone found some of the early Blevins men in a camp with other "Long Hunters" in the Rock Castle Creek section of Kentucky in 1769, he learned that they had been there for five years.

Some members of this early family migrated southward along the Big South Fork River and into the rugged and isolated mountains of Scott and Fentress Counties, Tennessee, in an area called home by such notable people as Sergeant Alvin C. York, Secretary of State Cordell Hull, Senator Howard Baker, and the parents of Mark Twain. The people of Scott County were loyal to the national government, and when the state of Tennessee seceded from the Union in 1861, Scott County forthwith seceded from the state. When the state challenged this action, the county officials informed them that they (Scott County) had as much right to secede from the state as the state had to secede from the Union.

At the beginning of World War I the people of Scott County, through their duly elected legislative body (the County Court) declared war on Kaiser's Germany and all her allies. According to local historian Laccie Blevins, Scott County has never officially rejoined the state of Tennessee, nor have they ever signed a peace treaty with Germany or any of her allies.

It was near Leatherwood Ford on the Big South Fork of the Cumberland River, that I first met Oscar Blevins and his wife. They had no electricity, no telephone, and they carried all their water from a small spring a quarter mile from the house.

Oscar talked of the hogs he had just butchered and showed me where his turnips, cabbage, potatoes and apples were still buried in the garden, as crisp and fresh as when they were stored there weeks before. He voiced concern over the wildcats, foxes, and hawks that preyed upon his chicken flock, and worried about the deer that ate his garden stuff in early spring. It was as if one had turned back the calendar to the early days of the settlement of our country.

A few years prior to my visit, another writer, the late C. W. Hume, editor of the *McCreary County (Kentucky) Record* found Oscar's grandparents, Uncle Jake and Aunt Viannah Blevins living in even more primitive conditions. They lived in the old log house with their nine children and two of Jake's maiden sisters. Hume reported that the women spun and wove all the clothing they wore. They tanned their leather, made their own shoes, and were almost completely self-sufficient.

Because of the building of the Big South Fork National River and Recreation Area, Oscar's land and his ancestral home were acquired by the state and he had to move away. Among his relics were some quilts made from hand-spun and hand-woven material. Old and worn, they had been relegated to the use of covering the tobacco.

It is quite likely that Viannah Blevins, left, and/ or her two maiden sisters-in-law, Elitha and Nancy, made the Blevins quilt. Elitha, center, was born in 1839 and died in 1928. (Photograph courtesy of Oscar Blevins)

The quilt shown here is one of those that came from the old Blevins family log house, and dates to the early pioneer time. The striped, hand-woven portion is assumed to be the back, and the far less attractive patchwork side would then have been used as the top. The filling consists of rags. This is probably typical of quilts in various parts of the country during the frontier period. (Photographed at the Museum of Appalachia)

RUFUS ELEDGE'S ALL HANDWOVEN QUILT

Rufus Eledge's quilt doubtless required more hours to make than any other one included herein because both the top and the back are made from handspun and handwoven material. Not only did every thread have to be spun on the crude spinning wheel and then woven one by one on the loom, but the steps in preparing and processing the material before spinning were simply prodigious.

Old timers said that it took at least sixteen months to produce linen fiber. The preparation of the seed bed was initiated in the fall of the year by turning the soil. The flax seed was planted in early spring, and the crop had to be cultivated and weeded throughout the summer until it matured in late summer, or early autumn. It was then pulled and seeded. It was allowed to "ret" most of the winter, and then it had to be cleaned, re-dried, broken, swingled, and "hackled" several times in order to remove the woody shell portion from every tiny stalk.

Cotton had to have every one of the multitudinous seeds removed. Wool had to have the cocklebur and begger lice pulled out by hand, and it had to be washed thoroughly. It has been said that it took ten times as long to spin thread for a blanket as it did to weave it, and that it took ten times as long to prepare the fiber as it did to spin it. So, several hundred hours were required just to make the cloth for a single quilt.

One of the many steps in spinning was carding, a process involving rolling the fiber into fluffy ropes by the use of hand cards. These cards each have hundreds of wire-like members and are common today in antique shops. The cards are simple devices, and it seems strange that every household would not have had at least one pair for use in spinning as well as for making the batting for quilts, but this apparently was not the case as the following excerpt from the diary of Amanda McDowell illustrates. Amanda, alluded to earlier, was from a prominent and well-to-do family in middle Tennessee. The fact that her father did not own a pair of cards is most revealing. Amanda and her sisters spun almost daily, and she spoke often of making quilts. This entry was made during the midst of the Civil War, hence her comments relative to the Army and the refugees.

Monday, August 3, 1863

I went to Mr. Cash's today and got a little wool. Tried to get a pair of cotton cards at Stones's, but the girls are fixing for a big quilting and had not made their bats yet. We can get them in a day or two. We cannot hear anything from the army. I guess we can hear when Mr. Sugart comes back, if he ever does. Most of the refugees have returned. I guess they feel a little ashamed of themselves. Mrs. Stones says, "The wicked flee when no man persueth."

Further substantiation that the task of making cloth from "scratch" was a continual struggle is found in another excerpt from Amanda's diary dated December 31, 1863.

The old year is going out in a storm. What a contrast this night is to four years ago! There were eight of us here and a merry crowd we were too, and tonight Mary and Ann carding and spinning, Father doing nothing, I knitting and thinking. Only three of us here tonight that were here that night. One, A. E. C., is in his grave, or at least is dead, for I do not know whether he was buried or not. Poor fellow, dead and almost forgotten. Perhaps his widow ready to marry again by this time! He did not even have a wife then.

The exasperation caused by the constant and monotonous tasks associated with making cloth was well put in Amanda's diary on Tuesday, October 13, 1864:

We have got our wool ready ... at last, Oh! I am getting so tired picking, coloring, carding, spinning, &c., I would secede from it if I could conveniently. I ought to write to Jimmy tonight but I have got no pen fit to write with. But I must write sometime. I wish I knew some remedy for laziness.

The Rufus Eledge quilt was acquired in the early 1960's from Rufus and Kellie Eledge who lived near the Smoky Mountains in Sevier County, Tennessee. At the time, Kellie and Rufus still lived in the old log house her ancestors, the Williams, built when they came into that wilderness area. There were eight log structures in addition to the house, one of which was called a loom house. It was in this early log house that the old "spinsters" of the family spent so many long winter days spinning, weaving, and quilting. The quilt came from this loom house along with many other quilts and coverlets. This quilt is 70" x 74" and has a wool inner lining.

LUTHER GRAVES OF BULL RUN CREEK

"This was one of mother's old quilts; all wore out but it does all right fer a dog bed. That's Grant's old dog, and the last thing he ever said to me before he died was, 'Luther, take care of my dog.' He thought the world of that ole dog. That's about all he had — no children, ner no property. Just his dog and them two ole trunks I let you have. I've took care of his dog. Got that old quilt fer him to sleep on. He don't want fer nothin."

THE DOG BED QUILT

"This here old quilt comes in handy when the fire dies down, and when that north wind gets up. Sort of like a lap robe," comments Luther Graves.

He is shown in the little three-room house he built for himself over a period of years. His twenty-five brothers and sisters have died, one by one, as has Luther's wife. Since his bachelor brother Grant died, Luther lives alone on his few acres near Bull Run Creek in north Knox County, Tennessee. The patchwork quilt he holds on his lap is one of many from a stack in a corner of his back room — all heavily worn after many decades of use. Luther and his quilts are discussed more fully in Chapter VI.

Chapter II

Use of Quilts Through the Years

When we think of quilts, our first and perhaps only association is in connection with bed coverings. While this has been, and continues to be, the most common use in this country, there are numerous other purposes for which they have been used through the years.

In most of the pioneer homes pine torches, open grease-burning lamps, or candles were the only sources of light. To be assured that some live coals would remain in the fireplace throughout the night, the fire was banked, or covered with bark or ashes when the last person went to bed. Virtually no heat was generated during the night, and the temperature inside these poorly insulated homes soon fell to within a few degrees of the outside temperature.

It is true that the feather bed was commonly used, but the quilt was the primary means for keeping warm on cold nights. Each quilt consisted of three layers, a most efficient insulation technique which is employed widely in our modern society.

The number of quilts used on a bed would vary, depending upon the weather, the thickness, the material used, and the number of people sleeping together. It was.not at all uncommon for five or six children to sleep in the same bed.

The number of quilts used on a single bed in the winter usually ranged from three to nine. Patricia Cooper and Norma Buford, in their book *The Quilters: Women and Domestic Art,* give an account of a school teacher in the Midwest who slept under twenty quilts in an endeavor to keep from freezing in the 13° below zero weather.

Buckskin and later handspun, handwoven hunting shirts were worn by men in place of coats in frontier times, and this custom continued into the late nineteenth century in some remote areas of Southern Appalachia. In extreme cold, quilts were sometimes used in place of coats they were unable to afford. Alex Stewart, the remarkable mountain man from Hancock County, Tennessee, recently discussed with me this interesting use of quilts:

> If they had a revival, they'd generally hold it (for) three weeks. People would wrap up in bed quilts or shawls and wade the snow five or six inches deep from the top of this ridge to the top o' that one over there to go to meetin'. Old grey-headed fellers with beards way down to here would be a settin' there wrapped up in quilts; more of a crowd than you could get there today. I've set there and looked at them a many a day and listened to the preacher preach. Old Vige Collins, he couldn't read ner write. He'd come down there and preach for them. Oh, boy! What a crowd he'd have. That man could preach! I've thought a heap about him.

Another common use for quilts was for pallets which were used in poorer homes where there were insufficient beds, or where beds were lacking altogether. The pallet was widely used in homes of all types when the numbers of visiting neighbors and relatives were more than the beds could accommodate. Ruth Stewart of Newman's Ridge in Hancock County remembers well the use of the pallet in her childhood home.

> We only had two rooms in our house, and with twelve children, if anybody come to stay all night, why some of us would have to make pallets. Mama kept two beds downstairs and three or four upstairs, and one in the kitchen, but if we had much company that wasn't enough. So, she'd spread some quilts down on the floor, put a feather bed on that, then some more quilts an' she'd have a pallet — sleep down there on the floor.

Ethel Hall, (a quilt maker from an isolated area near Viper, Kentucky, who is discussed at some length in Chapter V) also described the making of a pallet. There were eighteen children in her family, and she was asked if she had used pallets instead of beds.

Yes, sir. I'd have them (the children) to sleep right on a pallet. I had an old shuck bed back then — a big tick filled with corn shucks. I'd take that shuck bed and put it on the floor. Then I'd put some old sheets on that shuck bed and some quilts, and pillers made out of feathers. Them children would pile on there and there's where they slept.

The last time I slept on a quilt pallet was not altogether a pleasant one. When I was 13, the government forced us to move from our three hundred acre farm in the southwest part of Anderson County, Tennessee. This area came to be known as Oak Ridge, the government reservation where the major components for the atomic bomb were built. We had moved most of our grain, farm

THE PIECED TACK QUILT

Most tack quilts, or comforters, were made of large pieces of material with little or no regard for color schemes, patterns, or other aesthetic considerations. They were tacked every few inches, were made strictly for use, and were often poorly done at that. Perhaps this is the origin of the word "tacky" to denote shoddy workmanship.

This tack quilt however, has a subdued but pleasing color design, and is made of tiny triangular pieces of cloth tacked at close intervals. It has wool batting, and is believed to have been made about 1840 in Newport, Tennessee. It is now owned by Allison and Joe Arnold of Oak Ridge, Tennessee.

machinery, and the livestock to our new farm, but we hadn't moved our household chattels. To protect the items we had moved to our new home I was left as a guard there for a few days — until the rest of the family moved.

Since there were no furnishings in the new house, I spent that first night with Uncle Frank and Aunt Sophia Atkins who had moved to an adjoining farm and were living in a tiny four room house until they could build a permanent home. Since they had only one bedstead set up, it was decided I should sleep beside the stove on a pallet.

The prospect of this sounded pretty exciting to me, and I watched as my Aunt Sophia carefully made the necessary arrangements. First, she put a few layers of newspaper on the floor, then a couple of faded and slightly ragged quilts, followed by two more quilts for cover. With the addition of a

THE BARTER QUILT

Through the years quilts have been used for trading, bartering for goods or services, and they were sometimes used as a means of payment for debts.

When hard times came to the Robertson family of Eagleville, Tennessee, they were extended credit for a protracted period of time by the Arnolds, who ran the local country store. Mrs. Robertson made this quilt for the Arnolds as partial payment for the unpaid account. It is variously called Amish Star, Rainbow Star, and Prairie Star. It remains in the possession of Joe Arnold of Oak Ridge, the son of the store operators.

pillow, the bed was ready. She placed some more quilts in a near-by chair for after the fire died down.

The first few hours on the pallet were most comfortable, but I awakened some time during the night to a totally dark room. The fire inside the stove appeared to be completely gone. The room had grown cold, and I started to search for the extra quilts which Aunt Sophia had so thoughtfully laid out for me. As I did so, I heard a low, warning growl from Wilkey, Uncle Frank's dog. I remained silent for a few minutes, but as I became colder I again reached out, gently feeling for the quilts. Again Wilkey, from somewhere in the darkened room, gave a long rumbling growl like he meant business.

Again I stopped, and for what seemed like a half hour I shivered. My fright turned to anger and I vowed to find those quilts whether Wilkey liked it or not. I sat up defiantly and started to rise to my feet in a "damn the torpedo..."attitude. It was at this point that Wilkey sprang to his feet with such speed that I could hear his toenails scraping and scratching on the linoleum. In this dungeon-dark room he opened up with the most ferocious snarling, growling, and barking I have ever heard from a dog. I eased back down in my pallet and remained there, shivering underneath the two thin quilts throughout the long night.

In extremely cold weather, quilts which had become worn were often used as "windbreaks" in drafty cabins. They were even used on the floors as carpets. An unnamed traveler in the mountains near the Georgia - North Carolina border described these uses.

> When night overtook me I had not reached my destination, which was a visit to a hand spinner living two or three miles beyond the end of the road in country difficult to reach even in daylight. An old but beautiful cabin stood near the road and here I asked if I might spend the night. After a good supper and a visit around the fireplace, I was directed to my bedroom above the living room, commonly called the loft. When I had climbed the crude stairway the light of my candle revealed the whole sleeping apartment floor covered with beautiful patchwork quilts and, neatly hanging from the roof beams the entire length of the room and on both side of my bed, were coverlets and quilts to afford additional protection from any drafts, or rain, or snow which might come, and also, it seemed to me, to give splendor to the scene.

> These people had no carpets for their floor nor curtains for their windows, but they had a rare collection of home-made quilts, some of which were old and worn, but all I thought very beautiful and arranged in a way to create a royal room for the traveler who might drop in to spend the night. I could not walk over this carpet of quilts to my bed without first removing my shoes and by the candlelight that night I studied the designs and color combinations in perhaps ten or twelve of them. I doubt if I shall ever have the privilege of sleeping in such surroundings again, and if the sight of a patchwork quilt does not stir in me anything more than the recollection of the experience in this lovely scene it does quite enough. (Allen Eaton, *Handicrafts of the Southern Highlands,* 1937)

In literally hundreds of cases quilts, usually the old and worn ones, have been used in homes as a curtain-like covering over the inside doorways, especially during the winter months. In some cases these doorways had never been blessed with doors. In other cases, there were doors, but they were incapable of being closed — because of all the furniture, clothing and other items which had been placed in the path of the door swing.

The "quilt door" has a number of advantages. It does not require a large adjoining wall-space to be kept clear of household items, it affords quick and easy passage, there is no loud slamming, and it is usually more attractive than a plain wooden door.

When Ethel Hall was asked about the use of quilts for door coverings and for other uses, she laughed heartily.

> Law, I reckin I do recollect that. Yeah, I've done that — to keep the air out. Yeah, I've done that myself. Back before we had any doors, we used to hang 'em up over that one right there before we got doors to put right there. I have hung 'em over my windows too to keep air out. We've put them over our potatoes and stuff to keep 'em from freezin'. But I never did wrap up no canned stuff in 'em cause we dug a basement, we got a cellar down under here and we keep it crammed full of canned stuff, and we've got all our 'taters down there so we don't have to do that no more.

> We used to use quilts to cover up our 'backer before we quit raising it. Before he (her husband) got saved he sowed him a bed (of tobacco), and that was the purdiest

bed you ever seen. Well, when he took a notion to go to the Lord, he got saved, he said he just might as well take that and chew it hisself as to sell it to somebody else to chew. Said he felt like he'd be just as big a sinner hisself. So, he didn't raise it.

A most touching account of how quilts were used was described by Ethel. She was asked how she managed to work in the fields and supervise the raising of her corn crop on the steep, mountain land while at the same time raising six stepchildren and twelve of her own.

> I'd take my little babies out in the corn field where I's chopping corn when they's two weeks old. I'd take me an old quilt and spread it down under the shade somewhere. I'd lay the little feller down there and I'd put a cheesecloth over him when he's asleep to keep the flies and mosquitoes off — to keep them from biting the little feller. I've done that a many a time. Take me an old quilt and double it up, fold it up like me and you done out there on the porch a while ago. I'd come by every two hours to let him nurse, then I'd go back to workin' in the field — choppin' corn, diggin' out stumps or whatever else I's doing. They'd lay there and sleep all morning and all evening (afternoon).

> Back with the first children, we didn't have our roads up and down through here, and we'd take a horse and a sled and haul our little children, you know, to visit. And it'd be cold, and the little fellers didn't have no coat ner clothes hardly to wear, no shoes much, so I'd wrap 'em up in them quilts, put 'em in that sled and take off on my horse. I never would go off and leave my children with nobody. When I went, my young'uns went. If my young'un wasn't welcome, I wasn't, so I kept 'em home.

After this resolute mountain woman told me this story, it took a few minutes before the interview could continue. My mind was picturing a young mountain girl walking alongside the tiny farm sled, hitched to their only horse, with a half dozen of her small children piled in it. I could see the foot-deep mud trail that led out of this narrow mountain hollow, and the bright, curious eyes of those little children peeping from underneath the heavy quilts. In the dead of winter, I could see this devoted mother carrying her smallest ones, wrapped in the quilts, from the sled to the neighbor's house. I could see the older children barefoot, coatless and half naked, racing over the cold snowy ground toward the warmth of the log cabin. I wondered if those children would ever have had a chance to leave their log home during the long winters had it not been for the quilts that kept them covered.

Quilts were commonly made as wedding presents, gifts for cherished friends, and especially for children and grandchildren. Clemmie Pugh, for example, has given away all but a very few of the some four hundred fine quilts she has made in her eighty-six years of quiltmaking. Clemmie, who lives in Monterey, Tennessee, and is now past 100, is pictured and discussed in Chapter VI. Ida George, discussed in the same chapter, made sure she had a nice quilt laid back to give to every grandchild as a wedding present. In fact most old quiltmakers who were interviewed made their quilts with the idea that they would either be given away or passed on to their offspring or other family members.

Sometimes the old, tattered quilt was carefully washed and used as a padding in another quilt. Quilts too torn, tattered, and stringy to be used in one piece as an inner lining of another quilt were sometimes torn into small rags and used as a stuffing. This, of course, made the quilting process very difficult compared to sewing through fluffy cotton batting.

Odd as it may seem, one of the most common uses of old quilts in the Southern Appalachian mountains was for covering tobacco. In much of this region burley tobacco was, and is, the chief money crop of many small farmers. After the stalks are cut they are hung in open barns to dry for a couple of months. Once dried, the leaves will shatter like the black residue of a burned piece of paper unless one works with it on a rainy, damp day when the tobacco is in "case."

When the farmer finds tobacco in such pliable condition, he can pull the leaves from the stalks and pack them down in their dampened state so that they can be tied into "hands" and otherwise processed for market. In order to prevent these stacks of graded leaf from drying, they must be thoroughly covered, and that is where the old quilt comes into play.

Old quilts were often seen lying around tobacco barns. They would lie undisturbed all summer, often serving as a home for bumblebees (which love the cotton inner-lining). Year after year, when tobacco stripping started in October, these faded old quilts were again put to use. Some of them were so employed for a generation or two.

When indoor plumbing came into the rural areas, the task of "wrapping the water pipes" to keep them from freezing and bursting became a commonplace chore every fall. "Get some old quilts and

WANDA BYRD'S CRUCIFIXION TREE

Thirty-three year old Wanda Byrd of Walling Creek, a coal mining community in southeastern Kentucky, was anxious to talk about the quilt she had made. Wanda's Explanation of her crucifixion quilt discusses the symbolic Bible, the vine and branches, the church and the cross.

Well, Jesus died on the cross for the sins of the world, and faith comes by hearing the Word, so we go to church to hear the Word. And the Bible is the Word of God and the vine that goes around is where He says: 'I am the vine and you are the branches.' And we the Christians are the branches.

I have the Resurrection I want to do, and Jacob's Dream with the angels coming down and going up the ladder. There's a lot I want to do. I just want

to....when I go to church and I hear our pastor give a sermon I think how good that would look on a quilt. Because I think on a quilt it would witness to people. It would speak out. Because when people look at that, they know — maybe mostly only Christians; but it seems like everyone would know or would question as to why would He be hangin' there and why did He die? And He died for our sins and the sins of the world.

There is so much talent in quilting and I always wonder why isn't there something concerning the Lord when He's given us all these talents. And I thought that this is what I want to do for Him. I want Him to just use me in anyway He can that He may be glorified through my hands — through my work. I give him all the glory and the praise.

go wrap them pipes good" my mother would say, "it's going to get down cold tonight." In many cases these quilts were permanently wrapped around the pipes and remained there for many years as superior insulation.

Although canned fruits and vegetables (in glass fruit jars) were usually stored in a cellar or a dugout, they too had to be wrapped when the temperature would drop to below zero. Again the old quilts were the first choice. After the shelves of canned stuff had been covered, one last quilt would be attached to the inside of the door to prevent the cold air from sneaking through. Old quilts were also used to cover potatoes, which had to last from one season to another, and they were used to cover apples, turnips and other fruits and vegetables which could not be allowed to freeze. The use of old quilts became so popular in packing furniture and other household items that utility padded and quilted material is now made for that purpose.

The uses for old quilts are almost unending. When great-grandmother's quilt went through its second or third incarnation and became just too tattered and torn for any other purpose, it could always be used as the dog's bed... and a fine, warm dog bed it made. Old quilts seem never to die a sudden death. An old pair of shoes might be tossed into the trash can, but I don't remember seeing an old quilt disposed of in such a manner. They just keep being relegated to a lower use, until they are no more.

JETTIE SMITH'S QUILT WITHIN A QUILT

Dark was falling fast over the stark ridges of Anderson County, Tennessee, on a cold January afternoon. Robert Smith of Byrams Fork came forward carrying a big bucket of water. He had been to the spring, across the road at the foot of the ridge, to fetch water for drinking and cooking. He was asked if his wife Jettie ever made quilts.

"She's made a many a quilt" he laughed, "but she don't make 'em anymore. We can go in and see what she's got."

Inside the log house, Jettie was sitting by the coal burning stove in the single room in which they lived. The house had a second room but it had long ago been coverted to a storage room to replace the smokehouse and woodshed that had fallen down. The small room was warm, compact, and very

Jettie Smith is shown here patching a tack quilt she made when she first started housekeeping. "Well, I had an old hand-me-down quilt that belonged to my grandmother, and hit was plumb wore out. Well, I washed it out good and took and used it for the filler of this here quilt. Then I used feed sacks for the lining and scrap material to piece the top."

comfortable. It was as much room as they needed.

Jettie was the daughter of Tobe Hutcheson whose home was a few miles from where Robert and Jettie have spent their married life. "We wuz raised," Jettie said, "in what they called Poor Land Valley." When asked about her quilting, she replied. "Well, I started helping my mother quilt when I's about 8 years old. We'd quilt for people, and we charged by the spool. We'd charge a dollar for every spool of thread we used, and hit'd generally take us about a week to use up a spool of thread quilting that way."

Jettie was asked how many quilts she thought she had made. "Oh, I don't know how many I've made. Hit'd be a sight to see them if they was all in a pile."

A few days after this talk with Jettie, a lady from Ohio told me that she belonged to a club which did contract quilting and that their charge was twenty cents per yard of thread used, and that there was five hundred yards of thread in a spool. This would amount to $100.00, or one hundred times more than Jettie received for her sewing.

Jettie, who was born in 1912, continued to make quilts after she was grown, and until 1928 when she started working for Standard Knitting Mill in Knoxville. She worked six days per week, ten hours per day and received $16.00 for the sixty hour week. In comparison to what she had been getting for quilting, she felt that this was "good" money. Jettie worked in various cotton mills in the Knoxville area until 1943. Then she went back to quilting. She made three or four quilts each year for several years, but hasn't started one recently. Almost all of her quilts were made from animal feed sacks, flour sacks and scrap material. She has also used the little cloth tobacco sacks for the quilt backing.

THE QUILT AS A BEDSPREAD

In the winter of 1983 Lucy Stooksbury was the lone occupant of a rambling old farmhouse in the ridge country of Anderson County, Tennessee. In one of the back bedrooms, now seldom used, stood an unusual walnut bed made by her great-grandfather Hill. Upon this bed, serving as a bed cover or spread, was a fine old quilt made by Lucy's grandmother.

Lucy no longer used the room, the bed, or the quilt, so she sold the quilt and it was added to the collection at the Museum of Appalachia. When actress Jane Fonda visited the museum, she saw the quilt and asked to purchase it for her own use. Along with it she received an account of its history and a picture of Lucy standing by it.

This quilt, made in a small log cabin in the Tennessee mountains a hundred years ago, is indicative of the warm appeal American quilts have for so many people.

Lucy Stooksbury stands by the bed made by her great-grandfather and the quilt made by her grandmother.

Actress Jane Fonda at the Museum of Appalachia with the author and his wife.

THE QUILT AS A DOOR CURTAIN

When Mark Southerland, who lives in a one-room log cabin at the Museum of Appalachia, felt the cold wind whistling around the cracks of his door at night, he knew what to do. He got a quilt, the only possession he has which belonged to his grandmother, and hung it over the doorway. This is a technique that Mark had often observed in rural and isolated homes. It is very effective repelling drafts and adds a little color to the room.

Mark is completely obsessed with deer. He has collected over 3,800 photographs of them which fill several scrap books. The walls and ceiling are covered with pictures, cut mostly from magazines, of deer. Dozens of deer antlers hang both inside and outside the cabin. He is shown holding the head of a stuffed deer.

MARK SUNS HIS BED QUILT

A practice which Mark has often observed and has emulated is the airing of quilts. This is the one he uses as a cover, doubled over on his narrow bed. He stands in front of his cabin with a sheep and the famous nervous or fainting goats, named because of the manner in which they fall prostrate when suddenly frightened. After a minute or two they revive themselves and go about their grazing.

THE BEDSHEET
AND WASHTOWEL QUILT

A woman who had been confined to a mental institution in Nashville for over sixty-years — since she was a teenager — made numerous quilts, principally from bedsheets. She unraveled towels, wash cloths, and rags for the colored thread she used to create the various designs.

The staff didn't quite know what to do with her creations, so they sold them for a few dollars on behalf of the persevering quilter. Dr. Nat Winston, who served as the Tennessee Commissioner of Mental Health bought one and had all

but forgotten it until he had gone through his "good" quilts, then remembered having this one packed away.

Although each of the nine squares is different, there are similarities: the flag, people, and chickens. Nat remembered that the people were purported to represent doctors and nurses who treated the quilter, and that the relative size of their likeness on the quilt symbolized her regard for them. The institution included a farm, and this may explain her familiarity with chickens.

Chapter III

The Quilt as Folk Art

One of the basic, innate human traits is the desire to be remembered — and quite naturally, to be remembered in a fond and complimentary way. Perhaps that is one of the reasons people paint, build edifices, strive to be the president of the company, acquire a fine farm, have their pictures made, arrange to have a headstone erected, write their memoirs and make quilts. Few people like to think that their passing from this earth will go totally unnoticed or as the country song says, "with not a trace left behind."

The men in our society have traditonally had an opportunity, or at least a hope, that they would have a chance to leave some evidence of their existence; their farm, their business, the houses they had built, the chimneys they had laid, the devices they had invented, and most of all the children that bore their name. But the women could hope for no such remembrances. Until recently they could have little or no hope of leaving any reminders of their passage through this world. Very often the only kind of permanent recognition a woman got was through a beautiful and expertly sewn quilt.

Many quilts, especially in the early days of "housekeeping," were made purely for everyday use, and no pretense was made to make them pretty. They were among many on a bed, seldom seen, and used constantly until they were threadbare. After there were enough quilts to satisfy the needs of the family, the women could take the time for a more aesthetic and leisurely approach to quilt making. Instead of sewing the scraps of various sizes and colors together as they were randomly removed from the scrap bag, why not match the colors in some sort of a pleasing manner, perhaps even form them into some pattern? While sewing the three layers together, a practical and necessary chore, why not sew, or quilt, these stitches in an artful design?

During the evolutionary process of quilt making, the artistic aspect, both in piecing and in quilting, became more and more important. Eventually two practices developed. There was more emphasis, and more work, devoted to making a quilt beautiful than in making it serviceable. Secondly, some quilts were made exclusively for special occasions, for show, and for gifts. They were never intended for the beds of rowdy children, unbathed old men, or untrained unfants.

When our great-grandmothers made a beautiful quilt of this type and packed it away in their quilt chests, they had completed a work of art. They were not trained in color schemes, pattern creation, or needlework, and never even thought of the work as art, but they were true folk artists. Those hardworking housewives from the dirt-floored log houses of Kentucky, the windswept prairies of the eastern Dakotas, the sod houses of Kansas, the adobes of Arizona, and the lumber cabins of Oregon doubtless produced more true folk art than any other single group in this country's history. Nor were quilters confined to housewives in isolated and rural areas. Indeed some of the most exquisite quilts were made by wives of the affluent in the villages and urban centers.

The extent to which these old quilts have stood the test of time, the phenomenal nationwide interest in them, the heretofore unheard of prices, and their use as decorative items in some of the country's most tastefully decorated homes are tributes to the overworked housewives who designed and made them. They confidently recognized their beauty; but it has taken a couple of generations for their descendants to rediscover this beauty.

Rural America generally did not practice art for art's sake. Scholars argue as to why this is true, but in a land where there was a constant struggle to maintain the necessities of life, engaging in an activity merely to create something pretty was just not practical. Quilting fulfilled both needs. Making a quilt was an honorable thing to do, indeed, a necessary task. Who could be critical of one who, while making something so essential, also added some art in color or design. It is ironic that these women, in effect, had to bootleg, or sneak their beautiful art work into their quilts. There is no question that many, perhaps most, of their husbands would have forbidden them to have engaged in quilt making if they had thought the quilts were made purely for art's sake.

The point might be made that a quilt is not true folk art if it were based on a borrowed pattern, as was most often the case. Many knowledgeable quilters will be quick to point out that the vast differences in the color scheme, the adaptation of the pattern, the border, and dozens of little things that reveal the creativity and the artistic qualities of the quilter, are sufficient to put even this type quilt into the category of folk art.

Carter Houck, editorial director of the magazine *Lady's Circle Patchwork Quilts* states that "Out of frugality and necessity, the great American piecework quilt, our true folk art was born..." Dr. Robert Bishop, author of several books related to quilts and to folk art, says; "Almost from the day it was finished, a quilt or sampler was admired and treasured. Little wonder, for the best handmade American textiles were not only masterfully executed and functional, but are considered works of art."

Not only are quilts now being recognized as works of art, but perhaps for the first time in our country's history, they are being treated as such. In the April 1983 issue of the magazine *Metropolitan Life,* the cover page called attention to a story of folk art. The very first folk art object shown, more prominently than any other in this article, was an old quilt.

Two ingredients of folk art are the pleasing aspect of the object and the homemade, self-styled and personal manner in which it was made. Eliot Wigginton, editor of the *Foxfire* books once stated: "A quilt is something human. Quilts were handmade by people for people. Every phase of their production was permeated by giving and sharing."

There is a long-standing argument over whether or not fine quilts should actually be used. For a long time the daughters-in-law, nieces, and grandchildren ridiculed poor old Aunt Sally for keeping her beautiful treasures stored away in an upstairs chest. What an absurd practice, the younger folk thought. Aunt Sally was viewed as being a little peculiar and maybe a little senile. True, she readily showed her quilts to prospective admirers, and to members of the family. She would even use them on a few occasions — at Christmas, for a wedding, or when some family member died, but otherwise they lay folded neatly in the walnut chest that was older even than the quilts.

"If you don't ever use them," the popular and repetitious question to Aunt Sally was, "then what good are they?" And the question it seems, is not without merit.

But if Aunt Sally, and millions of her ilk, had not so carefully stored and preserved these treasures of the past; if she, and her comrades had used them on a daily basis as they were encouraged to do, these treasures would not be around for us to admire today. If they had been made solely for use and comfort, and been needed for that purpose, then it would have been foolish not have used them. But if, on the other hand, they were works of art, as Aunt Sally thought but didn't verbalize, then she was right in preserving them.

The contents of the following Will illustrates, in a most profound way, how much one lady thought of her quilts. The Will was discovered by Mrs. Lewis F. (Marjorie) Parsly of Oak Ridge while searching for geneological records in the Anderson County Courthouse in Clinton, Tennessee.

> In the Name of God Amen.
>
> I Nancy Yarnell of the county of Anderson and state of Tennessee being of sound mind and compasing memory and considering the uncertainty of this Mortal Life, knowing that it is appointed unto all, once to die do make and publish this my last Will and testament hereby revoking all others heretofore made by me in the words and figures following: Viz: In the first place I Will that all my just debts be paid (if any). In the second place I Will to Nancy Malinda Yarnell one Masail quilt and one German Rose coverlid, I also Will to Joseph Samuel Yarnell one patched quilt and one Twenty-five Snowball coverlid, The remainder of all my estate both real and personal, I Will to my sister Elizabeth Yarnell during her life, and after death to her heirs and in order that this Will be lawfully executed I appoint Robert M. Yarnell my Executor to execute this my last Will and testament whereof I have hereunto set my hand and affixed my Seal this 27th of May 1876,
>
> her
Nancy   X   Yarnell
mark

It is highly interesting to note that Nancy chose to make arrangements for the disposition of her quilts even before she designated who was to be the recipient of her real estate, which is believed to have consisted of forty acres and a dwelling house. It may also be noted that she mentioned no personal possessions other than her quilts and her coverlets. Nancy was apparently unable to read or write, as she signed her name with an "X", which was her "mark."

Almost all old quilts, and some not so old, may be considered to have some or all the elements necessary to qualify them as folk art. Hence the inclusion of certain quilts in this chapter is quite arbitrary. If folk art consists of personal artistic expressions of the common people, done by "folk" with no formal training, then the quilts included herein qualify, but so would many others found throughout the book.

The old Yarnell log house as it appears today.

EARL BLACKWELL'S HISTORIC QUILTS

When Earl Blackwell was disabled with advanced emphysema, he took up wood carving, stone sculpturing, and quilting. Like most so-called folk artists, Earl could give no clue as to what prompted him to take up such an avocation, except that he liked to be doing something. Even when he became so weak and short of breath that he was confined to bed, Earl was busy at something. As a matter of fact, most of his quilt work was done as he lay propped up in his bed.

In later years, Earl lived at the foot of Cumberland Mountain near the town of Jacksboro, Campbell County, Tennessee, but he was born in Clairfield, a most remote coal mining section of that county on the Kentucky line. His father started working in the coal mines at age 12, and was disabled at 45 because of "Miner's Asthma" or black lung. Earl worked as a miner, farmer, and trucker. He also worked for the coal companies in non-mining activities in Tennessee and in infamous "Bloody" Harlan County, Kentucky.

Earl spent four months completing each of these quilts, using a type of liquid embroidery. His wife then spent three months quilting each one.

There are literally dozens of symbols relating to the state, the federal government, and to southern Appalachian culture on the Bicentennial quilt. Included are the United States and the Tennessee flags, the American bald eagle, the state flower, the state tree, and state bird, and such indigenous things as a log cabin, a wash kettle, a rail fence, a hog eating acorns, overalls hanging on the line, and many more.

The Trees and Lake quilt may represent Norris lake, which is located only a few miles from where Earl once lived. The fascinating feature of this quilt is that the forest is composed of different kinds of trees and the leaves of each are remarkably similar to the actual leaves of the trees which they represent. To the casual observer, the leaves may appear to be the same, just as various trees in a forest may appear indistinguishable one from another. To a person who knows trees, however, there are realistic and distinguishable differences.

Earl identified the following trees on the quilt: magnolia, chestnut oak, cottonwood, walnut, sweet gum, white oak, weeping willow, elm, cedar, two chestnut trees with chestnuts, hickory, buckeye, and a pawpaw tree. Earl died about 1979, but more recently Mrs. Blackwell explained why Earl decided to make the quilts, and what prompted the various artwork. "Well, he just picked it up. He didn't have nothing to go by when he was a drawing all them things. He just had the idea in his head."

Earl Blackwell's Bicentennial quilt

The late Earl Blackwell, creator of two unusual folkart quilts, is shown in his home near Jacksboro, Tennessee holding a miniature log house he had completed. It is quite similar to the one on his Bicentennial quilt. He holds one of the windows to show that the lower section can be raised and lowered.

The Trees and Lake quilt by Earl Blackwell

THE HANGING ELEPHANT QUILT

While searching for quilts in Unicoi County, (which may be the most mountainous in Tennessee), my friend and venerable historian Pat Alderman found a photograph of a quilt called the Hanging Elephant quilt. It consists of twenty squares, each made by a member of the Senior Citizens Club to represent a memorable event in the life of the maker. The Hanging Elephant name was taken from one of the squares which depicts an elephant being hanged, one of the more exciting events to have taken place in the town of Erwin (see the detail picture of this square).

Pat remembered that the quilt was raffled and won by a woman named Ramsey whom he thought lived somewhere up on Indian Fork Creek. With that information, we set out to find the Elephant quilt. After numerous inquiries we found Ruby Ramsey who had the much talked about Hanging Elephant quilt.

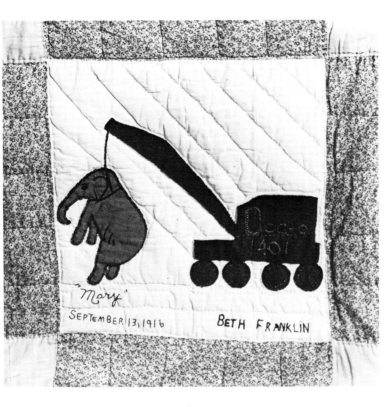

When a circus elephant named Mary killed her second human near Erwin, Tennessee in 1916, she was condemned to die. There were no guns big enough to safely and effectively do the job. Therefore, Mary was brought to Erwin where a large railroad derrick was used to publicly hang the killer elephant.

Bonnie Gentry, who is the niece of Holland Higgins, records a bit of history in her quilt square. Higgins was alledgedly killed by David "Hog" Greer, a wild hermit who lived in a cave in Unicoi County, Tennessee, near the North Carolina line. Hog Greer was himself shot and killed in 1834.

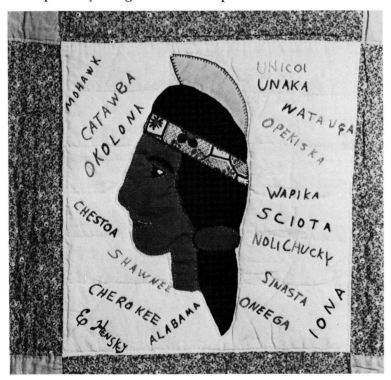

Mrs. E. Hensley records all the Indian names found in the small mountain county of Unicoi.

This graphic bit of folk art represents the quilter's memories of her early childhood.

SALLIE HASSON'S MASONIC QUILT

This most unusual quilt including scores of expertly executed Masonic emblems and symbols was made by Sallie E. Hasson, a member of a prominent East Tennessee family. Sallie was born in 1848 and is believed to have made this quilt about 1870. It was signed by her on the quilt top. She lived in Rogersville, one of the oldest towns in Tennessee. Her brother, Charles S. Hasson, served as president of the House-Hasson Hardware Company, one of the south's largest wholesale hardware houses. The old House-Hasson building was used as the headquarters for the administrative staff for the 1982 World's Fair.

Although the characters on the quilt are borrowed from the Masons' established set of symbols, their size, color, and layout are the folk art of the quilter. (Collection of Joan Self, Knoxville.)

ARIZONA DESERT SPRING

Myrtle Bessie Scott Nellis of Ash Fork, Arizona, made this quilt in the early 1930's and according to family also designed it. Maryann Mulvenon, who is shown with her husband's grandmother's quilt, asked the author to give it an appropriate name since it was an original design and had never been named. The design is reminiscent of the floral color of Arizona in the spring — hence, "Arizona Desert Spring."

Myrtle left Connersville, Indiana, in a covered wagon with her family in 1890, at the age of 7, and migrated to Salt Lake City, Utah.

After a short stay there, the family moved to Los Angeles, California, later to Williams, Arizona, and finally a few miles west on route 66 to Ash Fork, Arizona, where Myrtle married and raised her family. Myrtle was a school teacher and interested in art, as reflected in the design and color combination of the appliqued quilt. *Grandmother's Flower Garden* quilt was also made by Myrtle in the early 1930's and is held by Maryann Mulvenon, wife of Myrtle's grandson.

RUBY DAYTON'S
UNFINISHED FOLK ART QUILT

The little blue jeans which Ruby Dayton's two boys wore became so much a part of them that she couldn't bring herself to discard them. After they were worn threadbare, she found a few areas which remained in relatively good condition and with these pieces of material she started an Overall Quilt. Her boys, Clay and Carmon, helped her clip out various designs with which to decorate the quilt. They chose cars, boats, airplanes and such, while Ruby's selections were mostly flowers.

The quilt is a continuing project, and is not yet completed. A younger son, Melburn was born and his worn blue jeans were later added. He also is helping select decorative objects for the quilt.

Although Ruby has made several quilts, she is best known as an artist, emphasizing scenes from her native Appalachia.

One of the purposes of annual folklife festivals is to recall, explain and promote the arts, crafts, and customs of the past. One means of accomplishing this goal is making a quilt "from the ground up," so the children can observe the various stages.

At the Adrian Burnett Elementary School in Knox County, Tennessee, a quilt was made of forty-six squares, each square made by a teacher, school secretary, custodian or lunch-room worker. Symbols from school related activities and from everyday life are included. With the quilt is Vickie Wells, a teacher who has helped promote the folklife festival there.

GRANNY IRWIN'S CHRISTMAS QUILT

Granny Irwin was one of two girls in a family with eleven children. Her sister, a good deal older, married and left home when Granny was young. Hence, she and her mother cooked, washed, sewed, and otherwise did the "woman's" work for her nine brothers and her father. They also did the milking, much of the gardening, and the canning and drying of all the food. Granny was a prodigious worker, even in her eighties, and had little time for frilly, artsy things. It was surprising to find this purely aesthetic Christmas quilt which she had made. Perhaps she would have done more of this type work if time had permitted.

Her son shown here, later commented, "I always though it was the prettiest quilt I ever saw. But the only time she ever used it was around Christmas time. She'd get it out a few days before Christmas and use it as a bed cover til around the first of the year; then she'd put it away for another year. She made it, I think, about the time she was married in the late

1890's."

The embroidered subjects on this typical Victorian crazy quilt are in relatively high relief and include animals and familiar items found on the farm homestead where Granny Irwin lived. The Lord's Prayer is symbolically featured as the central motif. There is a dog, a butterfly, a horse, a bird, a goose and chickens, including a colorful and strutting rooster. Granny always liked music, so it wasn't surprising to find a fiddle and a Jews harp. There are several names and initials of the young women who may have helped make it. There is a "God Bless Our Family" inscription and a terse, revealing, and somewhat sad sentiment expressed in two simple words: "Remember Me." No one who ever knew Granny Irwin, who was called "Aunt Sarah" by all who knew her, could ever forget her — the jolly, energetic little lady who literally spent her life doing for others.

Chapter IV

Quilt Types and Patterns

It is commonly stated that there are two basic types of quilts; the pieced and the appliqued, but this simplistic definition gets to be somewhat confusing. Some quilts include both the pieced and the appliqued technique, and some so-called quilts, such as the tacked quilt or comforter, have neither. There are also numerous sub-types.

It is generally accepted that the common practice of using bits and pieces of used clothing, or scraps from the making of new clothing, gave rise to the name patchwork. The fact that the "pieces" were sewn together to form the quilt top classifies it as a "pieced" quilt.

Since clothing was much scarcer in colonial America than in the European countries, it is only natural that this practice of using scrap material was given new impetus here. So much so that some assumed this technique was initiated in America. But, as noted in Chapter I, the patchwork quilt, while popularized in America, is known to have existed in various European countries long before it gained popularity here.

The following quilt patterns and quilt types were selected at random, and are not necessarily the best-known or most popular. Here, examples of striking, beautiful, and expertly made quilts, appear along with dull, worn, ragged, and poorly made quilts.

The patterns are identified by whatever name the maker or owner used because the local names should be recorded. In many cases the more common or "proper" name is also provided. Identical or similar patterns may have several names.

The names of quilt patterns are both interesting and informative about the people, their culture, and even their sense of humor. Religious names such as Garden of Eden, Job's Tears, Crown and Thorns, David and Goliath, and Tents of Armageddon are expressive and poetical. Frontier inspired names like the Double Bitted Axe, Log Cabin, Saw Tooth, The Anvil, Bear's Paw, Barn Raising, Churn Dash and Indian Hatchet are reminders to us of the commonplace scenes of our great-grandmothers. There are historic names such as Burgoyne's Surrender, Lincoln's Platform, Courthouse Square, Nelson's Victory, King's Crown, and Sherman's March. There are colorful names like Arkansas Traveler, Drunkards' Path, Attic Window, Aunt Dinah's Delight, Cats Cradle, Broken Dishes, and Old Maid's Puzzle. Then there are names reminiscent of the old countries: Irish Chain, Dresden Plate, Dutch Mill, French Bouquet, and London Road.

In many cases there is a direct relationship between the quilt pattern and the name; Grandmother's Flower Garden, for example. One can look at this quilt and immediately equate the name with the pattern. Some, such as the Drunkard's Path, require more imagination. Some quilt names, such as Rob Peter to Pay Paul, have little to do with the actual pattern.

ELIZABETH WELSH'S BRIDAL QUILT

This most unusual Bridal Album quilt was made in 1872 in Charleston, West Virginia, as a wedding present for Elizabeth Welsh. It contains fifty-six blocks made by twenty-five of Elizabeth's friends and relatives. Each of the twenty-five contributors signed her name in India ink. One of the signatures was that of Elizabeth B. Welsh, the 90 year old grand-mother of the bride. Most of the blocks are also dated.

Allison Arnold who owns the quilt points out that it contains most of the techniques used in quilting. They include: piecing, applique, reverse applique, trapunto, quilting, and embroidery. The patterns were based on paper cut-outs, and most of them are believed to be original designs.

GRANDPA RICE'S FRIENDSHIP QUILT

A friendship quilt was made for Grandpa Rice about 1888 by unmarried girls in Big Valley, Union County, Tennessee. The girls spent a good deal of their spare time making quilts for the unmarried, but eligible, young men in the community. Each girl would make a square, embroider her name upon it, and incorporate it into a quilt. Over a period of time they had made a number of these quilts, enough, it was said, for every young man in the immediate area - except for Marcellus Moss Rice.

He was younger than the other boys and not quite old enough for marriage (The girls may have been concentrating on the more marriageable men). The young men who had received their quilts noted that Grandpa had not gotten one and "made fun" of him because the girls had ostensibly left him out.

When the girls learned that Marcellus was being ridiculed, they got busy and made him not just one, but two friendship quilts, the second one no doubt as an admonishment to the other boys who had thoughtlessly embarrassed him. He cared for them through the years, and eventually gave one to each of his two daughters, Ruby Rice Little and Ruth Rice Irwin.

The making of friendship quilts was quite common in most areas of Southern Appalachia, as well as throughout the country. This all-pieced quilt, measuring 81" x 60" with squares set on the diamond, has been called the Lily pattern and is generally called Tulip in Vase. Although there are three tulips in each vase, the singular form is used.

THE BEST OF SHOW

This adaptation of the Rose of Sharon pattern was made in the Civil War period by a member of the John Blair family who came from Charleston, South Carolina, to settle near the historic town of Kingston, Roane County, Tennessee. John Blair was a tanner and owned three hundred and fifty acres of land upon which his tanning and farming operations were conducted. The original homeplace contains only three of the thirty-six original log buildings once used as the smokehouse, buggy house, crib, barns, loom house, tannery, hen house, workshop, grainery, dwelling house, etc. Ap-

parently this had been a very prosperous homestead, a place where one would expect to find a fine quilt such as this.

The quilt may have been made by John's wife, Mary Johnson Blair who was born 1813, or possibly by one of their daughters: Mary Ann, Elizabeth Jane, Susan Caroline, or Nancy. The Blair sisters were noted for their dexterity in spinning, weaving and sewing.

Mary Johnson Browning inherited the quilt and recently entered it in the Old Quilt category at the Museum of Appalachia Quilt Show where it was awarded Best of Show.

DELLA McNEIL'S FRIENDSHIP QUILT
(The Friendship Ring)

The traditional story behind this quilt reveals that Della McNeil from the Fentress-Overton County section of Tennessee decided to make a quilt for a crippled boy in the community. Various women in the area volunteered to each make a square, and they subsequently placed their initials on their respective squares. The quilt was presented to the bed-ridden youngster when it was completed, but because it was so colorful and pretty he was never allowed to use it. It was kept packed away so that it would not be soiled or damaged. This quilt, called the Friendship Ring, measures 72" x 72".

JAMESTOWN, KANSAS
FRIENDSHIP QUILT

Andrea Fritts, left, and Margaret Heaton hold a friendship or album quilt made in 1870 for Margaret's grandmother Gray of Jamestown, Kansas. Margaret recalls that each block was made and signed by a member of the Methodist Church. The various appliqued patterns were dyed, Margaret had been told, with turkey-red dye. Apparently some of the women were not too adept at dyeing or perhaps the dye was faulty, because some of the blocks have faded appreciably.

GRANDMOTHER'S KANSAS
FLOWER GARDEN

Made on the plains of Kansas, in Cloud
County by Olive Gray, this Grandmother's
Flower Garden has an irregular border which
varies from the sides to the ends. It was pieced
from scraps left from the making of dresses,
aprons, etc.

THE BEAR'S PAW FRIENDSHIP QUILT
(with deliberate flaws)

Why did Sarry Turner's Bear's Paw have blue toes? And why were the toes on Elizabeth Herrell's Bear's Paw turned backward? These and other mysteries make this Friendship Quilt an interesting one.

The quilt was made in the Alder Springs section of Union County, Tennessee, and contains twenty squares. Nineteen of the squares contain women's names. Since only one man's name appears, that of Henry Lee Turner, one wonders if the quilt was not made for him. However, there are four double hearts in each square, one pair in each corner, and this may indicate that it was a wedding quilt for one of the girls. The speculation is that the girl for whom it was intended was Augusta E. Turner, since hers was the only square that was dated.

Four of the squares are blue, apparently dyed with indigo. These squares are signed respectively by Sarah Turner Johnson and her three daughters, Gertrude, Lodena, and Nola. Sarah's husband George was the youngest brother of Hannah Johnson Wyrick who was the great-great-grandmother of Namuni Young who now owns the quilt. She is shown holding it. Namuni bought the quilt at public auction at Halls Cross Roads, only a few miles from Alder Springs where it was made one hundred years previously.

The sixteen brown squares are believed to have been dyed with walnut hulls. The sqaure made by Elizabeth Herrell has the toes turned backward. The squares with the patterns are pieced, and the white squares contain a beautiful quilted pattern of feathered wreaths as well as the double hearts in each corner.

How does one explain the blue toes, and the backward toes? There was a common belief, adhered to by many, that to make a quilt too fancy and too perfect would be to tempt God. The Bible clearly points out our imperfection; to ensure that everyone knew he was imperfect, quilters sometimes deliberately created a flaw, such as the blue toes and the backward toes.

BALTIMORE ALBUM QUILT

This album quilt, which Mildred Locke uses as a wall hanging periodically, came from an old Tennessee home but was doubtless made in Baltimore. Mildred Locke and her quilts are discussed extensively in Chapter VIII. It is signed and dated in several places, and one inscription in the lower right hand corner reads: "Julia Ann Pentz, Pitt St., Baltimore City, 1847." Mildred points out that no two blocks on this quilt are alike and the workmanship shows at least five different makers. It is believed to be a presentation gift for a man because several of the blocks have men's names in them.

On the trunk in the corner are two antique quilts — a Crazy Quilt and a Log Cabin quilt, both made of silks and velvets. On the rocker is a Basket quilt made in Kentucky around 1880.

ALBUM QUILT

During the mid 1800's the Album quilt gained wide-spread popularity in many parts of the country. It consisted of a series of squares, each made by a different member of the family or community. These squares were then sewn together to form the quilt top, and quilting was done in the usual fashion.

Presumably the term "album quilt" is derived from the fact that various women contributed a portion, and because the respective squares often represented some place, event or object. Remembrance and autograph "albums" were also popular during the nineteenth century when the Album quilt was gaining popularity. Many authorities use the terms "album quilt" and "friendship" interchangeably, but it seems that "friendship" and "autograph" ought to be reserved for quilts where blocks are signed by different quilters.

The so-called Baltimore Album quilts are the most popular and sought after of this type. The development of these well known, exquisitely made quilts is credited to a group of Methodist women who were active in Baltimore, Maryland, in the 1840's.

OVERALL TACK QUILT

Even if Uncle Jake's overalls were worn threadbare in the seat and knees there were always a few areas where the cloth was strong enough to make quilt pieces — the lower part of the legs perhaps, and especially underneath the pocket covers. Close observation of the top portion of this quilt reveals the outline of the hip pocket from a pair of overalls.

The inner lining of this comforter, or tack quilt, consists of an old woolen blanket. The overalls accompanying the quilt are the type used in making the quilt.

One might think that quilts of this type would be relatively common in the Southern Appalachian region where most of the rural men wore overalls, but such is not the case. Only a few have been encountered. This one has a few wool patches and was acquired from the old Rufus and Kellie Eledge place near Bearwallow Mountain in Sevier County, Tennessee. It measures 78" x 63".

THE COMFORTER OR TACK QUILT

In showing her quilts, most any lady of the house will bring out the colorful pieced quilts which once belonged to her grandmother, the beautiful appliqued ones, and the Victorian crazy quilts. Sometimes, if you insist that you would like to see *all* her quilts, she will bring out the utility patchwork quilts made from dress scraps. She will almost never hand over the heavy comforter or tacked quilt. As a matter of fact, they are usually stacked and stored separately from the other quilts — as if she doesn't want them to be associated with her "good" quilts. As has been mentioned earlier, the comforter is not a quilt in the technical sense since it is "tied" or "tacked" instead of being quilted. The ties occur only every few inches and do not keep the cotton filling from migrating and becoming "bunched up." Many comforters had fillings of worn-out quilts, coverlets, and scraps of heavy cloth, and were so thick and heavy they could not have been quilted even if time had permitted.

The tendency to ignore this type of quilt is understandable for it can hardly be classified as beautiful, or even attractive. Most books on the subject of quilting ignore them altogether. However, from the standpoint of popularity and use, this type of bed covering was one of the most common. This was especially true in pioneer times, and in poorer homes of a later period.

With a half dozen beds, each requiring four to eight quilts, the women of the house could ill-afford to spend their time worrying about the appearance of the bed coverings. One could make several tack quilts in the time it takes to make an expertly quilted one. Opal Hatmaker, whose interview is included in Chapter V, stated that she, her sister, and her mother could tack a comforter in two or three hours, whereas it would have taken several days for them to quilt it.

Most of the older women with whom we talked learned to sew as small children, helping their mothers make comforters. When the family was no longer expanding and they had made enough "everyday" quilts, the mother, with the help of the girls, often started making more pieced, and even appliqued, quilts. Very often when a girl of limited means married, she would have to revert back to the tack quilt, or pieced quilts made from old woolen or colorless clothes. Under more prosperous circumstances, the young bride would be given beautiful appliqued quilts as part of her dowry. In some cases the bride would have a hope chest which included several quilts.

More of the old tacked comforters were made in the growing up years of our country than is generally recognized. There are not many shown from this period today for several reasons. First, as noted above, they are seldom displayed. Second, these were used on a daily basis and over a period of many years even these sturdy articles eventually wore out.

The word comforter, in some sections of the country, refers to a thick bed covering filled with feathers, straw, cornshucks, etc. In the areas we investigated, such items are called feather beds, straw ticks, etc., and not comforters.

THE TRAPUNTO, OR STUFFED QUILT

Trapunto is the name applied to quilting with designs stuffed or padded to create a high relief or three dimensional effect. Researchers say this practice probably originated in the 1400's in Sicily, where expert needlework has long been practiced. The art of trapunto was practiced in other European countries as well, and was apparently brought to America by early colonists, but these stuffed quilts were not nearly as well known here as were the other techniques.

In the classic way of making a trapunto, or stuffed quilt, the cotton or wool was inserted from the back of the quilt, by means of separating the threads and forming a tiny opening. After the stuffing had been inserted into the design, the threads were returned to their natural position.

The few I have found in the Southern Appalachian region were made in a different manner, according to family members. If they were appliqueing a grape, for example, they would leave a half inch area unsewn. Then, they would push their stuffing through this opening to create the raised design, and finish sewing or appliqueing the grape design on the quilt. In some cases they merely placed a wad of cotton on the quilt top, placed the designed fabric on top of the cotton, tacked it temporarily to hold it secure, and then attached the appliqued piece.

ROSE OF SHARON
(The Watermelon Quilt with Trapunto)

Beverly Burbage, a retired lawyer from the Tennessee Valley Authority, owns this beautiful quilt. Although Beverly is an authority on several categories of antiques, he makes no pretense to being an authority on quilts. He called this his Watermelon Quilt because of what appear to be slices of red-ripe watermelons which make up the quilt's border.

It is appliqued and has trapunto work, or stuffing, in the border. Beverly purchased it in the 1930's from an old German family, the Bargers, whose farm adjoined Beverly's father's farm in the Hillcrest Community, Sullivan County, in upper East Tennessee. Beverly recalls the elders saying that it was hand dyed and that it was made by Maria Barger, whose initials appear on the back. It is believed to have been made in the mid-1800's. The direct route from this area of Tennessee up the Valley of Virginia and into Pennsylvania probably explains what some would consider to be Pennsylvania characteristics.

THE CRAZY QUILT

The crazy quilt was one of the types commonly used in nineteenth-century America. Cloth was extremely scarce, so every tiny and irregular scrap was saved. In order to gain the maximum use of the available cloth, these variously shaped pieces were simply sewn together. The pattern was jagged, highly irregular and "crazy" looking. During the late 1800's Americans adopted more colorful, ornate, and decorative styles. Houses, furniture, picture frames, and many of the other articles produced during this time were ornate, sometimes to the point of gaudiness.

Frontier conditions were passing, the country was recovering from the devastation of the Civil War, and industrialization was expanding at a rapid rate. While the people were gaining more leisure time, they no longer had to think strictly in drab, utilitarian terms, but could spend time on the frilly, the fancy, and the colorful. This philosophy was incorporated into every aspect of their lives — including their quilts.

Hence, the fad of the Victorian crazy quilt developed. It was essentially the same type as the pioneer article, except that now they were made of expensive textiles with bright and varied colors. The crazy quilt was occasionally used as a bed covering on Sunday and was even used in the parlor. It was sometimes called a couch throw or a slumber robe.

In addition to being characterized by bright colors and odd shaped pieces of silk, velvet, and other fine cloth, the Victorian crazy quilt usually included fancy and ornate stitching using such techniques as herringbone, buttonhole, French knot, loops and diamonds, and feather stitching. Odd and unusual materials were often included. For example, some crazy quilts were made totally or in part from such items as campaign ribbons, silk shoe labels, labels from garments, etc.

Some observers feel the advent of the Victorian crazy quilt marked the end of the beautiful, minutely pieced and appliqued quilts of the previous years, called by some "the glorious period of quilting." They see the brightly colored crazy quilt as a degenerate, gaudy form, and have little or no respect for it.

Others feel this type of quilt respresents a very important mood and art-form in our country's history, and should be as carefully collected, studied, and preserved as the others types. Beauty, they would say, is in the eye of the beholder.

GRANNY IRWIN'S CRAZY QUILT
AND MATCHING PILLOW SHAMS

This Victorian crazy quilt was made by Sarah Jane Stooksbury Irwin of Union County, Tennessee. Her initials "S.J.S." are evidence that the quilt was made before she married in the 1890's. Several other names and initials appearing on the quilt are likely indicators that this quilt was the result of a joint effort. Maybe we should call it an "autograph, friendship, silk and satin, Victorian crazy quilt." The matching pillow shams were never completed, an indication that the quilt itself may never have been used.

GRANNY IRWIN'S BABY QUILT

Along with the completed crazy quilt found in a cedar chest at the old Kennedy place, there were 24 completed crazy squares which had never been sewn together, as well as various other squares that were never made into a quilt. The Dutch Doll baby quilt was made by my grandmother Sarah Jane Irwin and was passed around for use by her several grandchildren, including the writer. It was last used by my cousin Tommy Irwin, her youngest grandchild. It was to him that she gave the quilt. (Photographed at the Museum of Appalachia)

THE CRAZY, CRAZY QUILT

One would be hard pressed to find a crazier Victorian quilt than this one. Its composition includes the usual silk and satin pieces, plus clothing labels, campaign ribbons, and portions of mens' neckties. The symbols include scissors, hearts, a good luck horse shoe, and dozens of various types of flowers. It is signed, presumably by its maker, Lucy Knapp, age 77, 1887.

The James G. Blaine presidential campaign ribbon, the date, and the signature of the quilt maker provided rare documentation as the the age of this quilt.

THE APPLIQUED QUILT

The word applique is of French derivation and means to apply or lay on. Rather than sewing similar or variously shaped pieces together to form the quilt top, as in the case of the pieced quilt, the pattern of the appliqued quilt is sewn onto an existing top. The pieced quilt pattern tends to be designed in geometric forms while appliqued quilts have more varied motifs. There are floral, garden, fruit, and bird motifs, to mention a few.

The appliqued quilt became popular in most areas of the country in the mid 1800's and is characterized by its rich colors and beautiful designs. Many were made as show pieces, as gifts, and as heirlooms, rather than for everyday use. A surprisingly large number remain in pristine condition. As will be noted from the following examples, the style, designs, motifs, and color combinations vary widely.

WILD ROSE

Betty and Jack McDowell are shown at their home near Oak Ridge, Tennessee, with the Wild Rose Quilt made by Jack's great Aunt Mahala Rascoe of White County, Tennessee.

Mahala (1817-1907), who never married, made this quilt in the late 1800's. It is appliqued and has a trapunto, or stuffed, vine and grapes design on the two sides.

CHAPMAN FAMILY QUILT

This fine quilt came from one of Knox County, Tennesse's early and prominent families, the Chapmans. It is appliqued and is presumed to have been made by some of the Chapman women, probably in the late 1800's. (Collection of Joan Self, Knoxville)

SWEETWATER VALLEY QUILT

One would expect to find a striking quilt such as this in the beautiful and historic Sweetwater Valley which lies between Knoxville and Chattanooga, Tennessee. The appliqued pattern is somewhat similar to one version of Rose of Sharon, and the finely executed quilting design is of vases and flowers, with vines meandering throughout. It is owned by Namuni Young, shown here with her husband Harvey.

This California Rose quilt was made in Sweetwater Valley, one of East Tennessee's widest and most fertile valleys. The quilt was made near the town of Sweetwater, some fifty miles southwest of Knoxville. (Collection of Joan Self, Knoxville)

SUNBURST AND RIBBON

Lula May McDowell Stubblefield, who made this beautiful blue Sunburst and Ribbon quilt, won first place with it at the Tennessee State Fair in Nashville in 1963. Lula May's Aunt Mahala, who made the Wild Rose quilt shown above, lived with Lula May and her husband for many years and inspired her to appreciate quilts and quilting. This pieced and appliqued quilt was made in the 1950's near the middle Tennessee town of Sparta. Lula May was the aunt of Jack McDowell, shown holding the quilt with his wife Betty.

THE HAWAIIAN APPLIQUE

Jennie Snyder moved many times with her husband during his military career and the only place they stayed long enough for her to make a quilt, Jennie says, was Hawaii. It was there that she observed the unusual applique technique which she employed in making her own design for this quilt. Jennie was awarded a blue ribbon for the Best Appliqued Quilt in the 1983 Museum of Appalachia Quilt Show.

DUTCH DOLL

Few patterns were more popular than the Dutch Doll, perhaps because of the early Dutch influence on American quilting. This one was made by Ruth Rice Irwin as a young girl living with her parents on Bull Run Creek in Knox County, Tennessee, about 1922. It is pieced and appliqued, has embroidery on the bonnets, and measures 68" x 86". Our dog Freddie has no connection whatever with the quilt.

GRANNY RICE'S FEATHERED STAR
AND GRANDMOTHER RICE'S STAR-IN-STAR

Ruth Rice Irwin holds a type of Feathered Star her mother Ibbie Weaver Rice made about the time she started housekeeping in 1904 in Knox County, Tennessee. Granny was the eldest of sixteen children and helped manage the affairs of the family at an early age since her father was often away from home in connection with his duties as a Primitive Baptist preacher.

The quilt in the background was made by Ruth Irwin's grandmother Sarah (Sally) Longmire Rice, the daughter of a prominent farmer, Robert Longmire. They lived in Big Valley, Union County, Tennessee. Sally married Henry Rice who operated the well-known Rice waterpowered corn mill in Big Valley. This quilt has a Star-In-Star pattern. Both quilts are pieced.

NEW YORK BEAUTY

This, the largest old quilt that the writer has encountered, is slightly over nine feet square. It belongs to Mark King, at left, who acquired it from his mother, Mary Kate Farthing King, who in turn inherited it from her mother, whose maiden name was Lowry. She reportedly made the quilt about 1850 at the Lowry home in the Holston Valley section of Sullivan County, Tennessee, near where the state joins Virginia and North Carolina. Mark stated that it was used very sparingly through the years as a bedspread for special occasions or for special company. He, like other quilt connoisseurs, is at a loss as to why it was made so large, many years before the advent of queen and king size beds. It is all pieced and has very close stitching. The pattern, according to Mark, is Tennessee Beauty, more commonly called New York Beauty. The beauty at right, helping hold the quilt, is Brian Cullity, Mark's friend and fellow antique trader.

When Bernice Hensley (see pages 127 & 128), the quilting widow from Indian Fork of Unicoi County, Tennessee, pulled a quilt for her upstairs quilt chest, I immediately was struck with the fact that it was the same pattern as the large quilt belonging to Mark King. This one was made on the Priest River in Idaho by Bernice Hensley's grandmother. I soon learned, however, that her grandmother was a native of the same area in Sullivan County, Tennessee where the King quilt originated.

"She migrated to Idaho and she made this quilt for Daddy (Levi Hensley.) She died out there and my daddy come back to Tennessee and he brought this quilt with him. They called it the Bristol Beauty, or the Tennessee Beauty. I reckon since it was made in Idaho, it could be called the Idaho Beauty". The pattern is most commonly called the New York Beauty.

Mark King's New York Beauty.

IDA TURNER GEORGE'S QUILT

Ida Turner George always made and kept a few extra quilts on hand for Christmas presents, and especially for wedding presents for her grandchildren. The one shown here was made at her home in Union County, Tennessee, and presented to her granddaughter Willie Stooksbury when she married Morrell Irwin. This fancy Dresden Plate is pieced and appliqued, and measures 57" x 72".

KATE STOOKSBURY'S
DOUBLE WEDDING RING QUILT

Kate George Stooksbury the daughter of Ida George, always raised a patch of cotton for making quilts, according to her daughter Willie. As a child in the late 1930,s, I remember going to her house with my family and several neighbors to celebrate the coming of the New Year. As we waited for the midnight hour, we seeded Kate's home-grown cotton which was spread in front of the open fire. The seeds had to be warm before they could be picked from the tenacious fibers.

This popular Double Wedding Ring quilt was made by Kate about the same time as the New Year's Eve party — in the late 1930's. The home of Lawrence and Kate Stooksbury was in a rural area at the time, but is now the site of the city of Oak Ridge, Tennessee. The quilt lining was made from feed sacks and the trademark is still visible: "100 lbs. net, 16%, Wesco Dairy Feed."

CAROLINA LILY
WITH DELIBERATE FLAW

Close observation of the second square from the bottom, on the left side of this quilt will reveal the intentional mistake, explained in connection with the Bear's Paw Friendship Quilt. The stem is not connected to the flower in this square, but it is properly connected on all the other squares.

This Carolina Lily quilt was purchased by Namuni Young at the public auction sale of Dan and Bertha Woods estate in the Gibbs community of north Knox County, Tennessee. It was made between 1890 and 1900. Shown holding the quilt with Namuni is her husband Harvey.

THE BROKEN, OR OPEN, STAR
(One-Bordered Quilt)

An unusual feature of this quilt is that it has only one border, which, upon serious consideration, makes a good bit of sense. When used on a bed with a solid headboard and a solid footboard, neither the top nor the bottom of the quilt can be seen. If the bed is positioned against a wall, as was often the case, then the border of the quilt would not show on the wall side. One border was all that was needed; why go to all the work to add the other three?

The Broken, or Open, Star quilt was made by a member of the Cain family an early and prominent family from the fashionable Kingston Pike section of Knoxville, Tennessee. It bears the letters "R.C." on the back, presumably the initials of one the the Cain ladies in the late 1800's.

THE TRIPLE IRISH CHAIN

The Slonaker family, from whom this quilt came, lived in the community of Telford, a few miles from Jonesboro, Tennessee's oldest town. The triple Irish Chain quilt is pieced and dated May 31, 1887. Very few quilts in the Southern Appalachian mountains were dated and signed, other than the friendship quilts. Less than one percent of the quilts had either initials or dates. Of course, the better made quilts were more apt to have such identifying marks. (Photographed at the Museum of Appalachia with the late evening sun shining through a knot hole in the overhang barn.)

GRANDMOTHER'S ENGAGEMENT RING

This pieced and appliqued quilt is so tastefully decorated, intricately quilted, and has little or no padding because it was intended for non-utilitarian use. It was made for its beauty — its art. The drapery border, the hearts and tassels, the appliqued heart clusters and the quilted harts throughout the design indicate that it probably was made as a wedding quilt. Called Grandmother's Engagement Ring, it was made in Blount County, Tennessee in the 1860-70's.

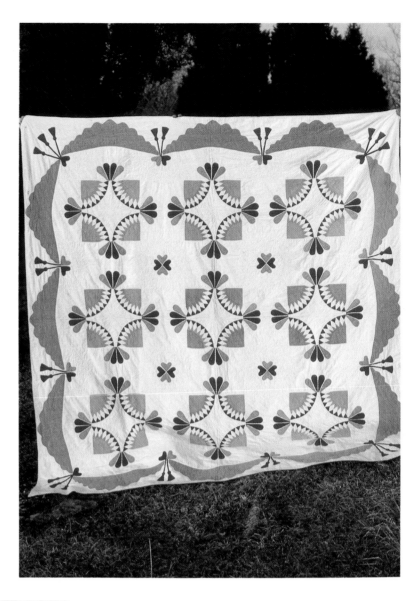

KUDZU IN THE CUMBERLAND GAP

The Cumberland Gap was probably the nation's best known and most important natural passageway through which early hunters and settlers passed in their westward movement. Located where the states of Tennessee, Kentucky and Virginia meet, it was popularized by Daniel Boone who is given credit for leading settlers into the new West — Kentucky, Indiana, Illinois, Missouri, and beyond.

The Cumberland Gap pattern is listed in *Tennessee Quilting* by Elwood, Tennery and Richardson, and was featured in the syndicated Nancy Cabot quilt pattern series printed in several newspapers in the 1930's and 1940's. This crib size quilt was made recently by Joyce Tennery, shown in the accompanying photograph, for her first grandchild, yet unborn. Although the pattern is from the original Cumberland Gap design Joyce added the word kudzu in the quilt name. Joyce choose the kudzu vine because of its prevalence around her home in Oak Ridge, Tennessee today. Active in local and state quilting organizations, she has taught her two teenage daughters to quilt.

IRIS BOUQUET
(A First Place Winner)

When Louise Cate of Knoxville married George Fowler, she gave up her teaching job to be with her husband who worked for the Federal Food and Drug Administration. (She did manage fourteen years of further teaching in New York, Michigan, Virginia, and Wisconsin.) After George retired and their three children had left home, Geroge and Louise came back to his ancestral home in Dutch Valley, Anderson County, Tennessee. This is a most beautiful valley, and the old Fowler place is one of the loveliest and most historic in the valley. It was only then that Louise started quilting.

Louise saw a picture of an Iris Bouquet pattern and made substantial changes in adapting it to suit her fancy. Flowers were left out of the corners, a border was placed around the central floral design, and other alterations were made. The new design won first place in the mixed techniques category at the Museum of Appalachia Quilt Show and Sale in the spring of 1983.

Like all quilters, Louise has enthusiasm for her work and looks forward to future projects. "I'm planning on making a quilt for each of my children, and including something symbolic from each of the eight states where we lived while they were growing up. It may take a while, but I'll sure have something to look forward to. Something to keep me busy."

BASKET OF FLOWERS

When Euretha Thomas was a girl in Campbell County, Tennessee, she often watched her mother quilt, but was not encouraged to join her because her mother did not want her fine quilts to be used for training purposes. When Euretha married Bruce Irwin in 1928 and moved into his family's old homeplace at the foot of Lone Mountain near Andersonville, her mother-in-law, Nora, had a quilt "set-up" before the fireplace in the large living room.

I told Grandma Irwin that I'd like to learn to quilt, and she said, 'Well, grab you a needle and go to work.' I started working on it and we finished that quilt and she took it to the fair in Clinton and won first place on it. And ever since I've been quilting off and on. I raised a family and worked for twenty-five years at the Atomic Energy Commission in Oak Ridge and at the Baptist Hospital in Knoxville. But I've quilted ever chance I've had — over fifty-two years. I wish I had one up now.

The quilt shown here was started by Euretha in 1936 and finished about two years later. She borrowed the pattern, Basket of Flowers, from her sister-in-law, Bonnie Irwin Carden. Euretha entered it in the Museum of Applachia quilt Show in March 1983, and won the Pride of Workmanship special award.

WILLIE KING GAUT'S QUILTS

Mrs. Willie Gaut is one of the many enjoyable folk from whom I purchased many early relics in the years when I first started collecting for the Museum of Appalachia. Extremely sharp, witty, and loving, she was nevertheless as shrewd a business woman as any mountain horse trader. In her younger days, she had been a collector of, and sometimes dealer in, fine early relics from Greene County, Tennessee. This is a rich farming area with a strong German influence, and an area which contained perhaps more quality antiques than any other section of the state.

I had never seen any of Willie's quilts, but I felt sure that she had some, and I knew they would be of high quality. I called her son King Gaut, who lives next door, and they readily invited us to stop for a look at their quilts.

Mrs. Gaut had moved from the old farm homeplace in the community of Bulls Gap to her present home in the shadow of Tusculum College, one of Tennessee's oldest institutions. Willie had some of her most cherished quilts out when we arrived. At 92, her dry wit and humor was as effusive as ever.

Willie King Gaut of Greeneville, Tennessee, and three of her fine appliqued quilts. The one shown on the left was made by her grandmother Annie Willoby Myers, from nearby Bulls Gap. The center quilt is from the Radar family who were among the first settlers in Hawkins County, around the time of the American Revolution. The quilt at the right came from her father's family, the Kings.

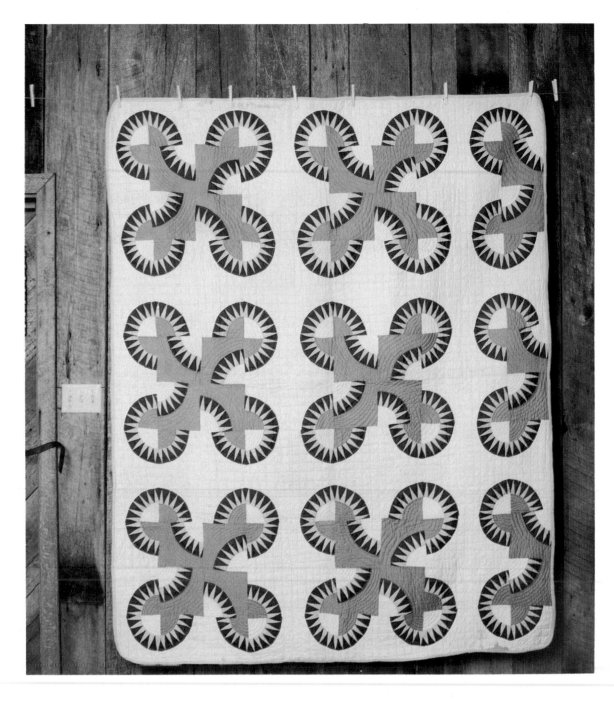

OPAL ROUSE'S GEORGIA RATTLESNAKE

"My mother-in-law, Rachel Rouse borrowed this pattern — they called it the Georgia Rattlesnake — from Jane Brummit who lived down here in Big Valley," Opal Stiner Rouse remembered. "I helped my mother-in-law quilt it. We worked on it, off and on, from 1926 to 1929. We bought the material for 10 cents a yard, and we grew our own cotton, seeded it, and carded it to make the batten.

"It was a hard job picking out all them seed. They used to put a big batch of cotton around the fire every night and have everbody to seed enough to fill his shoes. So the bigger feet you had, the more cotton you had to seed. Little fellers didn't have as much to do; but it took a mighty long time to seed enough to fill even a little shoe, especially when they packed it in. Later on we got a little home-made cotton gin, and that was a big help."

Opal, who is now 81, was asked when she started quilting, and how many quilts she had made during her lifetime. "Oh, gosh, I don't know how many quilts I've made. I couldn't begin to count - hundreds of them I guess. I started as soon as I was big enough to hold a needle. I guess I was 9 or 10 years old. We made them to use. Back then when you didn't have no heat in the bedrooms, it took a lot of quilts to keep warm. We wore a lot of them out. Then I've give a lot away."

Opal still lives in a remote section of Union County, Tennessee, where her ancestors settled in pioneer times. The community is known as Lead-Mine-Bend because of the lead deposits in that area, some of which were extracted and hauled out in wagons and on flatboats by her family, and others, a century ago. She was asked if she enjoyed quilting. "I sure do. I love it. I've quilted all my life, but I had to quit last year because my hands can't hold a small needle like you need to quilt."

JUDY ELWOOD WITH HER GRANDMOTHER'S LONE STAR QUILT

Judy Elwood is shown here with the Lone Star quilt made by her grandmother, Ida Weaver Handy of Anderson County, Tennessee. This is one of two Lone Star quilts made by Mrs. Handy. According to Judy, the many other quilts she made throughout her life were utility quilts made from scrap material.

Judy, who has a Bachelor's degree from the University of Tennessee in Textiles and Clothing, has now become hooked on quilts and quilting. She is a charter member of the Smoky Mountain Quilters Association and was largely responsible for organizing what has become the Annual Smoky Mountain Quilt Show. She is co-author of the book *Tennessee Quilting*.

THE LONE STAR
(From 5,024 Pieces)

If you have 5,024 tiny triangular shaped bits of cloth, a few months free time, and are skilled and dexterous of hand and mind, you can make yourself a quilt like the one shown here. If one were to remove the points of the star, he would have a great example of a spider's web. This Lone Star quilt was made in Hamblen County, Tennessee in the 1930's and is now owned by Lois Mahaffey of Powell, Tennessee.

The variation of the Texas Lone Star pattern, and of many other patterns, seems endless. This one was made by Pearl Cleveland who died at the age of 95 in the Graveston Community of Knox County, Tennessee. Juanita Hutchison, granddaughter of Mrs. Cleveland, is pictured with the quilt. It belongs to Juanita's daughter Leisa Hamilton, great-granddaughter of Pearl Cleveland.

FROM BOSTON TO MAINE TO TENNESSEE
(The Double "T")

When Charles and Margaret Sawyer were married in 1904, Margaret's Aunt Abby McPhail made this quilt for the Swayer's as a wedding present. Abby, who was an invalid living in Boston, was of Scottish descent and spent much of her time sewing and making quilts.

Charles and Margaret Sawyer, who lived in Sabattus, Maine, gave the quilt to their son and daughter-in-law, Allen and Edith Sawyer because of Edith's interest in quilts and quilting. Edith later gave the quilt to her daughter LeAnne Arnold, its present owner, who lived in Norris, Tennessee.

Knoxville artist Ruby Dayton is shown with her adaptation of the popular Log Cabin pattern quilt which she recently completed.

THE 1847 SARAH KARNS BLAZING SUN QUILT

According to family tradition, this quilt was made by Sarah Gammon Karns in 1847 for her daughter Mary, who was then four years of age. The Karns were one of Knoxville's oldest and best known families. They produced several notable citizens, including one mayor of the city. Frances Crippen Hilman is the great-granddaughter of Mary Karns, and the great-great-granddaughter of Sarah, who made the quilt. She is the present owner. She acquired it in 1929. It is pieced, and the quilting designs in the all-white squares are similar to the pattern on the pieced squares. The pattern is a type of Blazing Sun.

AUNT LIZZIE GRAVES

A few hundred yards before we reached Lizzie Graves' house, we could see a long line of brightly colored quilts, waving gently in the morning breeze. Her neighbor Jess Butcher had told me of this 92 year old quilter, and our visit couldn't have come at a more opportune time. At first this energetic little lady was somewhat reticent, but when we asked about her quilts and her quilting, she became talkative.

Everybody calls me Aunt Lizzie. Ain't nothing but Aunt Lizzie. My maiden name was Keck, and I was born in Claiborne County, Tennessee, close to the Union County line. They was eleven of us children, and I started making quilts when I's 12 years old.

My mother, she kept her frames rolled up to the ceiling when she wasn't a quilting — if she had up a quilt — 'cause the children would run against them and knock them first one way and then another, and it would mess them up. She kept them rolled up to the ceiling to where she could reach.

I was always counted a fairly good quilter, but then still they's a lot of people that can quilt better'n me. My mother-in-law was a whole lot better quilter than me. Her stitches, you couldn't tell 'em apart — they was all just exactly alike.

Just before I got married mother helped me make four quilts. She raised sheep for the wool, and then spun and wove it for the quilt backing. We called them linsey quilts. Yeah, I've shore enjoyed quilting, in the wintertime. In the summer I'm out working in the garden, gettin' in wood and such. But when cold weather comes I like to quilt.

"This red quilt was always called the Four Hands, and it was made by my husband's mother Sarah Jane Cook Graves," Lizzie remembered. "I guess she was the best quilter I ever knowed."

Sarah Jane Cook Graves, maker of the Four Hands quilt is shown standing at the right. Her sister Lizzie is beside her, and her mother "Granny" Haun Cook is seated. The two men are Sarah Jane's brothers.

Lucinda Angeline Pike Keck, Lizzie's mother, is shown here with husband Philip Keck, and their eleven children. Lizzie is the small girl at left on the front row. She and the other three girls were referred to as the four little ones.

THE CHIP AND WHETSTONE QUILT

Few articles were more commonplace in pioneer times and in rural America than the whetstone, or whetrock. Used to sharpen all household and farm-related tools, it was usually elongated in shape, often tapering on either end, not unlike the points of the stars in this quilt.

The whetstone was carried by the man of the house to sharpen his axe; for he was always chopping trees. Hundreds of times I have seen my grandfather sharpen his axe with his whetrock, then lay it beside a stump amidst piles of chips from the recently cut tree.

I don't know whether or not this type whetrock, and these type chips, are connected with the derivation of the quilt's name, but that's what I think of when I hear the name, Chips and Whetstone. The eight points of the star represent the whetstones, and the small pieces surrounding them are the chips: fresh-scented ash, oak, and hickory chips.

This quilt, believed to have been made about 1885, is from the W. B. Ballard home located in the historic Fort Sanders section of Knoxville. Ballard, who was a conductor on the Louisville and Nashville railroad, died in the 1930's.

BACHELOR'S DREAM

David Byrd lives in the picturesque mountain town of Erwin, Tennessee, and has spent his life as a trader of Appalachian artifacts. When I asked him about quilts, he brought this one from his "not-for-sale" room, describing it as the best quilt he ever bought. He didn't have definitive background information on it, but stated that it came from the upper East Tennessee, or Western North Carolina area. The people from whom he bought it called it Bachelor's Dream.

THE HANNAH REBECCA BLAZIER QUILT

The name of the pieced and appliqued pattern of this quilt is not known to the writer, but its unusual, intricately quilted design includes wreaths, hearts and crosses. It was made in the extreme eastern part of Tennessee, in Sevier County, near Great Smoky Mountains National Park. It is believed to have been made about 1878, and is signed by its maker, Hannah Rebecca Blazier. According to Al Dodson of Knoxville, owner of this interesting quilt, Hannah Rebecca Blazier came from Sevier County to the Kimberly Heights section of Knox County in a covered wagon in 1912. Al acquired the quilt from Dot Jones Plemmons, granddaughter of Hannah Blazier, maker of the quilt. (Photograph by Ed Meyer.)

PRIM ROSE AND RISING STAR

Bonnie Irwin Carden holds what she calls the Prim Rose and Rising Star pattern which she made about 1925. It was pieced in the old house shown in the photograph where she lived at that time and was quilted at her parents' nearby home.

Chapter V

Visiting Old Time Quilters

Some of my most memorable and rewarding experiences have occurred while visiting with a number of old time quilters. They varied greatly in age, background, and economic status; but at the same time they all had a great deal in common. Whether they were making quilts to sell, as presents, or for their own use, they all thoroughly and completely loved quilting. Flossie Cornett of Jeff, Kentucky, said, "Oh, Lord, I love it!" Ethel Hall of nearby Viper said, "I'd druther quilt than to eat on the hungriest day ever I seen."

All quilters emphasized the great joy and consolation which resulted from their quilting. Interestingly, most of those who expressed such enthusiasm tended to quilt alone. This is not to say they did not enjoy the social contact and the visitations. But it seems a person who enjoys quilting only with a group is not a true quilter. Much of the basic satisfaction of quilting comes from a successful effort to use imagination, ingenuity and hard work to create something of one's own.

The writer didn't talk with a single quilter who didn't seem happy and content, and so many of them were widows living alone. One may argue that only a contented, well-adjusted person would have the patience and perseverance to become a quilter in the first place, and that quilting itself did not contribute to their healthy state of mind. But quilting, like gardening, is great therapy. Psychiatrists might do well to study quilters with regard to the relationship between their art-craft and their exuberance for life and living.

If there is a universal trait shared by all, it may well be the pride and pleasure of creating. Even in completing such mundane tasks as weeding the flower bed, mowing the lawn, baking a cake, or cleaning a dirty oven, one has a sense of accomplishment and pride when one stands off and observes the completed job. How much more pride does one experience if the completed task is a work of great skill and art?

The manner in which a quilt is made can reveal a good deal about the personality, temperament, philosophy and general lifestyle of a person who made it. If one questions this premise, then he has but to examine and study the extraordinary workmanship and artistic attributes of some of the finer quilts made a hundred years ago — now commanding prices ranging into the thousands of dollars. Then he should examine some of the many polyester quilts being made today, priced as low as forty dollars each.

BONNIE CARDEN, ACTIVE QUILTER AT 86

Bonnie Irwin Carden is one of those people who looks the same today as she did thirty or forty years ago. A recent visit found her exuberant because she had just finished, after several weeks of labor, her latest quilt, an Endless Chain. She is 86 but, like most quilters, it seems to me, she appears many years younger in body, mind and spirit.

Bonnie, the daughter of Boss and Nora Irwin, was raised near the foot of Lone Mountain, a half mile off the public road from the village of Andersonville. When her mother left her quilting frame unattended, Bonnie would grab the needle and thimble and start quilting. "I would slip around the quilt when Mother was out, and I'd try and do as good a job as she did so she wouldn't know that I'd been quilting."

I asked her how old she was when she started this. "Well, I was a very small girl. I remember that I made my first dress when I was 9 years old; so I guess I was maybe 8 when I started slipping around and quilting."

Much of Bonnie's quilting has been for the weekly quiltings at the Andersonville Methodist church. The women charged a certain amount for quilting a quilt and donated the proceeds to the church. Once, Bonnie recalls, the group made a quilt themselves and sold it by means of a raffle for the benefit of the church. "Then," Bonnie said, "we began to get criticism from some other members that this was a form of gambling. That was the first and last time we ever raffled a quilt." When the church quilting ended in the late 1970's, Bonnie had been attending these weekly quilting bees for almost sixty years.

While many people her age have difficulty finding enough to occupy their time, Bonnie has difficulty finding enough time to do the things she enjoys. "It might be a little late in life to be so enthused about something like quilting, but I've just finished one and can hardly wait to get another one started."

WINNIE IRWIN'S ORIENTAL POPPY

This appliqued pattern was the work of a cousin, Winnie Irwin, and the quilting was done by her mother, Nora, sister Bonnie, and sister-in-law Euretha Irwin. The pattern is believed to have been taken from a magazine in the early 1940's.

EVA ROGERS CLAWSON
(A quilter for seventy-eight years)

Eva and Garfield Clawson live on the same farm where they started housekeeping over three quarters of a century ago. The home is located in the Speedwell, Tennessee, community near historic Cumberland Gap, and the old log house where they first lived is still standing — next to the white frame house where they now live. It cost them $100.00 when they built it sixty-seven years ago. Eva is 92 and Garfield is 97.

On a recent visit we found Eva busily working on her latest quilt top, and Garfield sitting on the porch chewing tobacco and enjoying the beauty of the lush, spring countryside. They were a most friendly and affable couple and responded eagerly, and often simultaneously, to my questions.

Q. Eva, tell me a little about your quilting and your life here in this community.

A. I've made quilts all through life. I've made all different kinds and done all kinds of fancy work, like embroidery, crocheting, and I've spun. I learned to spin on the big wheel. I've done all kinds of work. I said it's history to the young people to know how

Eva and Garfield Clawson sit on their front porch with one of the last of many hundreds of quilts she has made during her 93 years. This one now belongs to a neighbor, Mima Joyce Leach and was borrowed for the photograph since Eva has given away or sold all the quilts she has made.

we used to have to live.

Before our children got big enough to work, I went to the fields and pulled corn. We didn't have no fertilize back then, and he'd (Garfield) haul the manure out and pile it up, and I'd carry it in my old cotton apron, out to the hill and drop it by the side of every hill of corn. I've cut corn, I've cut t'backer (tobacco) I've graded t'backer, I've suckered t'backer, and I've raked hay, and I've done everything but plow. But after the children got big enough to work, I quit that. I had so many children — seven is a big bunch — it took something to put up enough food for them. I'd can four and five hundred cans a year. I had a big garden, and what it didn't take for the family, I'd sell it. Garfield hauled produce all the time. I'd raise chickens and I'd raise turkeys. I'd raise a thousand chickens a year. In World War II, I raised chickens and I got 65 cents a pound for 'em. I'd raise five hundred and when they was gone I'd raise five hundred more.

Q. Almost every old quilter that I've interviewed (I've talked with some that were over a hundred years old) enjoyed gardening. Do you like to garden?

A. Yes, yes. Why, I had an acre garden last year myself. And I filled my deep freeze just as long as I could put a thing in it. Canned my beans, and my tomatoes, and made my tomato juice. Why yes, I love to garden.

Q. Where were you born?

A. I was born just about a half mile up the road here. I was a Rogers. I'm the oldest of eleven. Six boys and five girls. I've just got one brother a livin'. He's 78 years old. Our folks was lawyers — on my side of the house — lawyers and doctors.

Q. Well, tell me about when you first remember seeing quilting done, and how old were you when you started quilting?

A. I was 17 years old when I got married and I was quiltin' long before then. Mother learned us to do everything. I could cook when we was married, and I could do embroidery work. I could do everything before I was married.

Q. Did your mother do a lot of quilting?

A. Oh, yes, she had to. She never did make quilts to sell. She quit after she got enough made for her family. She just gave us children four quilts apiece — that's all she give us.

Q. You mentioned the turkeys that you raised, and Garfield was telling about driving them to market. How do you go about driving a large flock of turkeys all the way to Tazewell?

A. Just bunch 'em up, about a thousand of 'em together, and put them in bunches. Get you a row of men and drive 'em, you know. You get too many together and they clog up. Take about a thousand and divide 'em up into about four or five bunches. You couldn't drive 'em now, — too many cars! They wasn't no cars back then when you drove turkeys. And we flew 'em across the river.

Q. How did you make them fly across the river?

A. If one flew, they'd all fly. If you crowd them along the bank and get one to fly across then here they all go flying across.

Q. Did you have to keep them on the road?

A. Yeah, keep 'em on the main road, and when night would come they'd go up and roost. Oh, they'd fly up. You couldn't drive 'em. We had about twelve hundred (turkeys) here one night, and had to have twelve men and boys to help drive them. Garfield would go around the country and buy turkeys from other farmers, and he'd keep them here in the barn until he had enough for a drive.

Q. Let's get back to quilting. What did you use for the filling in your quilts?

A. I raised cotton. I raised cotton right out there you know, and I learnt to card my batts, you see, to pad my quilts. I had a box that I knew just exactly how much it took to pad a quilt. Law, you talk about good quiltin' — that was so good. We had an old cotton gin, and you'd lay your cotton down in front of the fire and get it good and warm, and you run it through that cotton gin. It had a wheel on it. We gave our oldest son the one we had.

Q. How many quilts have you made over the years?

A. Well, I guess two thousand, I don't know for sure. Surely I've made that many in ninety-three years.

Q. Did you give a lot of them away?

A. Oh, yes. I give the children all twelve apiece — they's seven of them. Then I've got twenty-one grandchildren and I've give them all a quilt apiece. And all the granddaughters, I've made them all wedding quilts. And then I've made all the great-grandchildren quilts. I've been makin' quilts all these years.

Q. How long have you been selling quilts?

A. Well, you know what I've done? Mr. Moss, who was senator of Kentucky, well, they had a cabin that my brother built. He built them a house over here at Straight Branch Dock. They (the Senator and his wife) come over and stayed for the summer, and we got acquainted with them — awful nice people. And so, I's a quiltin' — I'd start in August quilting when I was able to quilt. And she come over and wanted to know if I'd sell some quilts. Oh, I had so many of them then stacked up. I said yes that I'd sell them, but I never had sold no quilts. You know Mr. Moss said to her, said: 'Now, you buy ever one you want.' Well, we went upstairs and she picked her out five, and do you know what I let her have them quilts?

Q. What?

A. Twenty dollars apiece — $20.00 and they just kept going up you know. I sold 'em for $40.00 for a good while, and then I sold 'em for $50.00. And now when I furnish everything, I've been a gettin' $150.00 fer 'em. And that's not enough.

Q. How long would it take you to make one?

A. Well, it would take from twelve to fourteen days. That's how long it took to quilt a quilt. So, now you make a quilt like I'm makin' now and it takes a month.

Q. Do you enjoy quilting?

A. Law yes! I reckon I do!

Q. Which do you like to do best, quilt or garden?

A. Well, I've always worked out, all my life even before I was married. Why you know I'd druther be out in the summertime workin' in the dirt.

Q. The winter was the time you did most of your quilting, I guess?

A. Yes, but in the afternoons, the way I do now, is to go out early of a mornin' and work til maybe nine o'clock, and then I'll come in. I'll do my housework and quilt during the day. Then I'll go out late in the afternoon and work 'til nine o'clock, in the cool of the day, you know. That's the way I make the garden.

Q. Well, you've been quilting a long time. You said, I believe, that you made your first quilt in that old log house when you were 17 — soon after you were married?

A. Yes, that's where we started. You know, we was married up the road here a little ways. And we come here (and moved in with his parents) and the next morning we got up at four o'clock. Well, Gar got up to go plow corn and I had to get up too! And it was a strange place, you know. Well, hit wasn't long til I was a helpin' to cook. I could make better bread than his mother could; better biscuits. I always have been a good hand to make biscuits. And it wasn't long til I took over the garden. Now she didn't work. She was just 45 years old, his mother was, when we was married, but she didn't work out like I've always worked. But Grandpa (Garfield's father) would help me.

Mother give me a sow and pigs and we raised them pigs and sold them for $15.00 and bought the first bedstead we ever had. And I picked the geese for feathers to make a feather bed.

Q. And you never had a honeymoon?

A. No, nothing. Never had a trip nowhere. Of course, I've been to Michigan. I had a sister that lived up there and I've been up there twice. That's the only place I've ever been.

Q. And this 75th anniversary celebration that you had on May 10, was that the first thing of that type you've ever had?

A. First thing we've ever had. Oh law, I did enjoy that! I just met so many of my friends that I hadn't seen in so long, you know. Girls, well they was younger than me, but they were good friends. I hadn't seen them in ten or fifteen year I don't guess.

Q. Whose idea was it to have the anniversary celebration?

A. Mine! (she chuckles) Course, I couldn't have had it if it hadn't been for my children. You know they just have everything. I've give every thing I've had to my children. And they just had everything pretty, and it was the nicest thing you ever saw. Poor Walt, that's my son-in-law, just carried all them pretty flowers. They have an awful nice home. She just has everything — silver, candelabras, silver trays, and everything and it was beautiful, the table was! Pretty tablecloths.

Q. Have you been sick much in your life? Have you been in the hospital much?

A. Never til the last four or five years. I broke my hip and that was my first time in the hospital.

Q. Were you in the hospital when the children were born?

A. No, had midwives with the three first ones. They was all born at home. We had midwives with the three girls. And you know, back then you sat on the husband's lap to have your babies.

Q. I've never heard that before.

A. That's the way it was. My first three children was born on my husband's lap. We had a mid-wife, Aunt Betty Hawn.

"We set up housekeeping in this old house over seventy-five years ago and we're still at it," Garfield laughingly states. "My Grandpa raised his family here, and I don't know how much older it is than that. It must be about two hundred years old."

Hundreds of quilts and her 93 years have not dampened Eva's enthusiasm for sewing and quilting. She is shown piecing a Dogwood Quilt top, and talking excitedly about how pretty it is going to be when it is finished.

QUILTER MARY CROSS
(100 YEARS OLD AND GOING STRONG)

Although Mary Shoopman Cross is well into her 101st year, she is as alert, talkative, and exuberant as a teenager. She was born in Overton County, Tennessee, but has lived most of her life in nearby Albany, Kentucky. She now alternately lives with her children, and was staying with her daughter Fannie Honeycutt in Knox County, Tennessee, when I talked with her. Her hearing was good, and her mind as "keen as a briar."

I's raised in a little log house. My daddy was a renter (tenant farmer), and we just moved from one farm to another. Had a big family, eight children, and he was sickly. He took sick while he was a soldier in the Civil War, and he never was well. The last real days work he ever done was the day I's born. We had it purdy rough.

The first glass lamp that ever come in Byrdtown, I got one of 'em. Well, I went to town and saw them lamps, and I went back and I begged my daddy and he give me money, 50 cents. I went back and got the glass lamp. Well, I thought I was rich. Oh, I

"I commenced piecing quilts when I's 8 years old" says 100-year-old Mary Cross. She is shown on the front porch of her daughter's house playing "Shortenin' Bread" on the harmonica and holding one of the last tack quilts she made.

thought I was rich with that glass lamp. It burnt coal oil.

Before that all the light we had was an old open grease lamp. You'd twist a little rag just as tight as you could twist it. And you'd get you some grease — hog lard — and put in a saucer, and you'd put that rag in there and let it hang off over here on the edge. Now that's what candles we had. The way we kept far (fire) was to get oak bark and build a little far up in the farplace, cover it up, and you could just keep far on and on.

I commenced piecing quilts when I was about 8 years old. Back when I's piecin' quilts, when I'd go anywhere, people would give me pieces of their dress to put in my quilt; why it would just tickle me to death. Had to save everything. Fannie, get that one and show him — the one that's made out of strings and pieced on paper. A little string that wouldn't be that big (she measures a quarter inch), you could piece them on paper and then tear the paper off when you went to set it together. Save ever little string — wouldn't throw away a little string as big as your little finger.

You asked me about quilting parties. If we had room enough, we'd put up three quilts at a time and really have a big one. I told Fannie the other day that if she'd have quiltin's now, she'd have room for four. (Mary laughs) Yeah, a whole bunch of people would come. And you know, Fannie, before she was grown, she'd go to 'em. And she took the brag name of being the nicest quilter. Made the little stitches.

When I asked Mary if she ever heard of the old custom of throwing a cat on the finished quilt, she laughed heartily and grabbed both my hands with hers to make sure I listened to her account of this practice.

Well, now they'd generally be two boys come in and two girls about the time you was gettin' ready to take the quilt out of the frame. And they'd catch the cat, and when they took the last thread out of the lacing, why they'd get at each end of the quilt and they'd throw the cat in there, and when the cat jumped out, the one closest to where he jumped out would be the one to marry first. They had a lot of fun thataway. Why, I've shook the cat myself! (she laughs)

Did I tell you what I used to use to make the quilt lining out of? I used to make them out of the old tablecloth — the oil tablecloths. You can take that old oil cloth and soak it in homemade soap, and roll it up and let it stay a little while. Then you can take a case knife and scrape ever bit of that oil off. And then you can color that lining. Course it was made out of the best factory (material) they was. And law, that there quilt lining would last for years and years and years.

During one of my visits with Mary, I asked her if she knew Hennie Copeland the old "granny" woman who lived near her early childhood home. Mary studied for a while and finally said: "No, I knowed some Copelands, but I didn't know her." Then, in a most parenthetical manner she said, "I was a midwife — a granny woman, you know?" I didn't know, but I soon learned that she had delivered babies for over three quarters of a century.

And I never had a speck of bad luck in my life. I was the only one there was in the neighborhood and it just kept me going all the time, you see. They'd give me a dollar, but lots of times I wouldn't take it — the people was so poor and I wouldn't take their dollar. A feller offered to pay me once. I saw that him and the children didn't have nothing on the table to eat but fried green tomatoes and cornbread; and I wouldn't take his money. I've delivered a heap of babies and not charge them a penny. I believe in helping people out. I commenced when I was young. I was 20 when I commenced and I went on up until the last ten years, I guess. I just quit going, I told 'em I was too old. I'd druther quit when the time was good, and I hadn't had no bad luck. I quit 'fore I had bad luck.

MARTHA McMAHAN, THE
STAND-UP QUILTER

If we were awarding a prize for the most unusual quilter, then Martha Shelton McMahan of Knox County, Tennessee, would surely take the blue ribbon. A widow and the mother of eighteen children, this tiny, eighty-three pound woman earns her living by making and selling quilts. She makes no pretense about artistic fulfillment or creativity, but candidly states that making quilts is the only way she has to pay her bills.

Martha was born near the North Carolina border, in Sevier County, Tennessee, and grew up on a farm beside Byrges Creek. One of eight children, she early learned to work in the fields as well as to perform the various household chores. She learned to quilt as a child by watching her mother make quilts to keep the family warm. Her mother, who is in her 90's, is still living.

In 1936, Martha married James Britton McMahan and they eventually moved to a tiny concrete block house on Neubert Springs Road, a few miles southeast of Knoxville. Her husband worked at odd jobs, as a "shade tree" mechanic, and collected and sold metal junk and cardboard. Martha explained that she often helped her husband.

> We'd pick up cardboard in the dumpsters and behind the stores twixt here and Kingston Pike in Knoxville. We sort of lived that way. Not perfect, but we got by. We'd work for several days to get a truck load, and hit'd bring from $18 to $22 dollars a load.

I asked Martha about her children — how many she had, where they were, etc. And I asked her, of course, about her quilting.

> Well, I've got fourteen children living, and four dead. I had 'em all at home. I didn't go to no doctors, and I never was in a hospital. I don't believe in hospitals. No, I sure don't.
>
> I had a granny woman most of the time. Lou Maples from Sevierville, I had her several times, and my husband's mother, she delivered one or two. And then a woman by the name of Lena Dare — she delivered some of 'em.
>
> My husband died four years ago the 20th of next month (February 1983), and all the children are gone from home. I've got one boy that lives close by and he comes through during the day and looks after me, fetches my wood and sees that I've got water in, and he takes me back and forth to the store to get my quilting material and such things.
>
> I quilted and sold some quilts when I's raisin' the family, but not too many. I've really been in the quilting business, I'd say, for the past six years. Makin' and sellin' quilts is the only income I have. I work from early in the morning — sometimes I start before 7 o'clock, and I work til late at night. I work sometimes til the television stations sign off. It's awful quite and peaceful out here then.

This brought us to an amazing discovery concerning Martha's quilting. I noticed there was no quilting frame in the house. Upon inquiry I learned she used neither a frame nor a hoop.

> I do all my quilting standing up. I lay it (the quilt) on the bed there and jest stoop over it and quilt. I quilt all day long and til late at night a standin' there. I never set down when I'm quilting. Now of course I set down when I'm piecing a quilt. But as far as setting down to quilt a quilt — I never do. Never used a frame — never had one.
>
> To get one right and everything, I can piece a quilt and put it together in a weeks time, if I work from early morning til late at night without stopping. And for the thin-backed ones I get $30, for double-backed one I get $40, and for the thick-backed ones I get $50. The baby quilts, they're always $15 each. By the time I buy my material, I'm not gettin' a heap for my work. But I like to quilt. It gives me something to do.

In the "front" room of her tiny house, Martha works on a quilt square surrounded by boxes of quilt scraps on her right, and by piles of finished quilts on her left.

The crude sign, the modest home, the outdoor privy with a painted door, and the attractive quilts on a sunny January day tell much of the story of quiltmaker Martha McMahan.

Martha McMahan, whose only income is from the quilts she makes and sells, never had a quilting frame. "I always do my quilting standing up. I work sixteen hours a day just stooped over the bed a quilting."

"This will make the eleventh quilt top I've made since my 100th birthday," Clemmie Pugh points out. "If I'm not working I lay down, and I shouldn't lay down too much."

This Butterfly Quilt is one of some four hundred quilts Clemmie Pugh has made over the past eighty-five years. This one was completed in her ninety-ninth year. "I've given all but a half dozen away. I never lost anything by giving things away." See story on the following page.

CLEMMIE PUGH, QUILTING
INTO HER SECOND CENTURY

Clementine Copeland Pugh was born in the mountains of Overton County, Tennessee, in a one-room log cabin, with puncheon floors, one door, and two glassless window openings. Red clay was daubed in the large cracks as partial protection against the cold winters, and a small rock chimney and fireplace provided the only heat. She was 100 years old on September 12, 1982, and in the five month period from that birthday and the time I talked with her she made ten quilt tops — all by hand. Her stitching, color design, and patterns are superb; "Clemmie," as her friends call her, is as alert, spry and agile as a woman half her age, and her sense of humor and joyous outlook on life are truly inspirational. She has quilted for almost ninety years and has made an estimated four hundred quilts.

I went to visit her in the middle Tennessee town of Monterey a few weeks before Clemmie's centennial birthday, but she wasn't at home. Concerned that she might be ill, or in the hospital, I went anxiously to the nearby home of Dow Pugh, one of her sons. "What day is this? Thursday?" He said. "Oh, yes, this is her card-playing day. She's walked down to one of her neighbors to play cards. She plays twice a week, no matter what. Even during last winter's big freeze, I had to go down and help her across the ice and snow. She used to whip me for playing cards, and now, her 100 years old, she plays twice a week!"

Clemmie's mother was a striking, resolute mountain woman known throughout the Cumberlands as Aunt Hennie Copeland, one of fourteen children raised to adulthood by Andrew Jackson Walker and his wife Clementine. Aunt Hennie was an herb doctor and a "granny" woman reputed to have delivered over 1,500 babies, often riding through the rugged and forested terrain during the night hours.

"Lord, I recollect a many a time some feller would wake her in the middle of the night. She'd put the side saddle on the old horse and away she'd go," Clemmie remembered. "Mother'd go whenever and wherever anybody asked her. She done it as a favor. Sometimes she'd get some hog meat, sometimes they'd give her half a dollar for deliverin' a baby; but lots of them folks was so poor they couldn't give nothing."

Clemmie's father Abraham Copeland seems to have been a more passive person, who was overshadowed by his energetic, ambitious wife. He was also a native of Overton County, where he and Aunt Hennie raised their eight children, including Clemmie, at a place called Sinking Cane.

In a recent letter to me, when Clemmie was well into her 101st year, her son Bill reflected upon his mother as a quilter:

> As you perhaps know, mother has made quilts ever since she was in her early teens; she was raised to work and keep busy. I well remember when all of her six sons were still at home, she had no less than 50 stacked up that she had made, and when each of her six sons married and left home, she gave each one 5 quilts.
>
> Since that time there is no telling just how many she has made and given to her children and others, and to my knowledge she has never received one red penny for them. In fact I sometimes get a little steamed up by her heartiness. And then too she could never say NO and people knowing this takes advantage of her.

On September 12, 1982, Clemmie's children and her friends sponsored a Clemmie Pugh Day in commemoration of her 100th birthday. Five hundred people gathered to honor this venerable lady.

I first came to know Clemmie through her son Dow. Dow went "north", to Battle Creek at age 16 and worked there for thirty-five years. After his wife died and his only son was killed in a bicycle accident, Dow returned home. But the old home place was gone. He bought the chimney, moved it to a site on a bluff near Monterey, and then, with the help of neighbors, built a cabin around his mother's old chimney. Dow started whittling, and has become one of the south's best known folk artists. I bought the first such art Dow ever sold, and after a few years I became acquainted with and progressively more intrigued with the Pugh family, including Clemmie whom I've called "Queen of the Cumberlands."

My most recent visit with Clemmie Pugh was February, 1983, when Robin Hood joined me for the purpose of photographing her and some of her quilts. Robin, anicipating a 100-year-old woman, was astounded by the fiesty little lady who greeted us at her door. As Robin took pictures, I turned on my recorder.

Q. Well, how are you feeling today, Clemmie?
A. Oh, I'm fine; it's my old knees and back that ain't much account. But I reckon I

do purty well for my age, for being 100 ever since the 12th of last September.

Q. We want to talk to you about your quilting. When did you start, who taught you, how many have you made, and what have you done with all of them?

A. My mother learnt me to quilt when I's just a young child. We'd work in the fields and gardens and when it was cold or rainy, we'd quilt, or spin and weave.

I've spun a many a day all day long. She'd card and I'd do the spinning. And she'd put the cloth in the loom and I'd weave it. I could weave a yard a day, of the fine thread, you know. Kept my foot a goin', and a throwin' that old-fashioned shuttle all day long. We all kept busy. We had to.

Mother had an old frame that hung from the ceiling. And the holes in the frame was burnt with burning irons. Didn't have no augers back then, you know. They'd just heat an iron poker or something in the fire and burn the holes. We kept it up all the time in the winter. Of course in the summer, we had outdoor work to do — canning and carrying on. And being ten in the family took a lot of cooking.

Q. Back then, did you use flour sacks, or fertilizer sacks, for making quilts?

A. No. We didn't have no sich back then. We'd take old worn-out pants, you know, and wash 'em, and make quilts out of the best parts of them. Then my mother bought brown domestic sometimes. But she raised her own cotton and we'd pick it. She'd card the cotton for the quilt filling, and for spinning too. She'd card and I'd spin and weave it.

We'd make towels out of cotton. We never had a store-bought towel all the time I's growing up. They were all made of old home-made stuff. And we had straw ticks and feather beds we slept on.

Why, Mother never made no fancy patterns much. Most of her quilting was for old everyday quilts to keep you warm. I started quilting some at home, when I's about 12 years old. But I didn't do so much quilting til after I's married -- in December 1900. I went to quilting right after I got married, soon as I got me enough material together, you know. And I've quilted ever year since except the year my husband got sick and died, in 1942. I had to look after him that year.

Q. You've been making quilts on your own since 1900. How many do you suppose you've made?

A. Well, I have no idea. I've give 'em all away as soon as I made 'em. I've made at least four or five a year, and I've done that since I got married 82 years ago; so figure it out for yourself.

Q. That would be over 400 quilts!

A. Well, I've made ever bit of that many. (Much laughter) I always kept a quilt on hand, and then when I'd set down to rest, you know, I take my work up and work on the quilt. And you know I never lost anything by giving things away. My husband said I gave a good living away. He didn't believe in working and giving it away, but I never lost anything by giving folks something. I never went hungry. I've give 'em to my children, my grandchildren, and my great-grandchildren, and my nieces, and to my friends.

I remember once I'd taken my husband's old pants, where the seat had wore out, and the knees, and ripped them up to make a quilt. And I took some of his old coats where the elbow had wore out, and some other old clothes, and I made a quilt. I had just finished it when my husband's brother's wife came by. Her name was Julie. She looked at me and she says, 'You give me that quilt, I need it and you don't.' She had a great big family too, and she didn't make quilts. And I just handed it over to her and she was the proudest thing! And we went there to stay all night sometime after that, I don't know how long, and she put that quilt on our bed and she says, 'There's the quilt you give me.'

Q. Did you ever sell a quilt?

A. No — yes, I take that back. Dow sold one for me a few years ago — sold a Turkey Track made out of red and green. (Dow was in the room with us listening to the conversation, and I couldn't resist asking....)

Q. Well, did Dow give you the money he got for the quilt?

A. (Clemmie laughs heartily) Yeah, he give me the money — my boys have all been good to me. I'm proud of my boys. That's the only thing I've got that I'm proud of is my children. My boys are just wonderful men. It's not becoming of me to brag on 'em, but.... (Clemmie was unable to finish the sentence — but she didn't have to.)

Q. Where do you get all the material to make the quilts?

A. All the people around here know I make quilts and they bring me their scraps. My niece up here brings me some. Why, material is $2.00 and over a yard! That pink and red stuff there is over $2.00 and somethin' a yard and I'm not a gonna pay that to make the quilts and give 'em away!

Q. I'm sitting here watching how fast you sew, and how you use the thimble. How old is the thimble?

A. (Much laughter from Clemmie) I've used this same thimble ever since I've been married.

Q. For eighty-two years! That's amazing.

A. Yeah, I had it when I was married and I've used it ever since. (laughs again)

Q. I understand that you haven't quilted any in the last few weeks.

A. No, I haven't quilted lately. My shoulder got to hurtin' and I couldn't quilt. But, I've made a lot of quilt tops this winter. I've made eight Double Wedding Rings and two Flower Gardens. And I'm working on another Flower Garden. I give them to Jimmie Mae here — she's my grandson's wife, you know. And I give them to my daughters-in-law. I've got to have something to do, and that's why I like makin' quilts so well. If I don't have something to work at with my hands, I'm layin' down, and I shouldn't lay down all the time.

Q. Well, since you started making quilts about eighty-eight years ago, you've only sold one quilt that you've made. I must say that it doesn't sound like you're a very good business woman?

A. No, I'm not. I'm no business woman. I'm just an old country woman living in town. (Laughter)

Clemmie, front row at left, is shown here with her father and six of her brothers. Her mother Hennie is standing directly behind her husband because she was expecting her eighth child and it was considered to be in extremely bad taste to have one's picture taken in such a "condition." The Copeland family members, front row, left to right are: Clemmie, Abraham, Herbert being held by his father, William, Perry, and Walter. In the back row are Jim, (mother) Hennie and Bob. This photograph, taken February 1, 1897, was made on the front porch of the log house where the family lived. (Photograph courtesy of Bill Pugh)

Although Clemmie has given away virtually all of the some four hundred quilts she has made over the past eighty-five years, she had a few packed away neatly in her bedroom. Among these is a most unusual one which she called the Church Quilt. I asked her to explain.

Well, we wanted to raise money for the church, and we made this quilt and everybody that wanted their name on it give us 15 cents. So, we made quite a lot of money out of it. All of us church women would get together and quilt. I made the batten out of home-grown cotton, you know, and put the cotton in and got everything ready, and the women come in and quilted.

Certain women would be responsible for a square and they'd put their name in the center of the circle; and they'd also be responsible for getting people to pay to have their names embroidered around that circle.

Twenty women were each responsible for a square. Their names appeared on the squares, in the center of the circle; and they'd be responsible for getting other people to pay to have their names embroidered around that circle. There are a total of three hundred and sixteen names throughout the quilt

Charged each one 15 cents to have their name put in, you know. You count the names on that at 15 cents, and that runs into a good bit of money. I give $10.00 for the quilt (at public auction) after it was finished - and that helped the church too. Why, I wouldn't take anything for this quilt. They's so many of them that's dead and gone.

I asked Clemmie where the actual quilting took place, what church it was for, and the year in which it was made.

I had it set up in my house and the women would come there. Look in the corner, the date's there — I think — yes, it was 1935. We done it for the Baptist church here in Monterey. We generally worked on it during the day. Us old women didn't get out too much of a night.

Clemmie's grandparents, Andrew Jackson Walker and wife Clementine Walker are shown here with their fourteen children. Clemmie's mother, the legendary Aunt Hennie Walker Copeland is shown at the extreme right of the second row. This is, family members state, the only time that all the children were ever together with their parents. The picture was taken about 1885. The members of the Walker family are identified as follows, from left to right, first row: Bill, Jim, Andrew Jackson (father), Clementine (mother), Susan, and Belle. In the second row are: Kate, Lou, Rosaione, Leann, Priscilla, and Henrietta (Hennie). In the third row are Jack, Joe, Bob, and Halla.

TYLER BUNCH THE QUILTER

Tyler Bunch is one of the most venerable and kindly of the many mountain men I have known. His home is in the isolated section of Hancock County, Tennessee, deemed by the United States Government a few years ago as being the third poorest county in the country.

The Bunch home is located in one of the most remote sections of the county, at the head of Snake Hollow, and near the community of Blackwater. Newman's Ridge towers over Snake Hollow and over the Bunch house. This area is the home of a mysterious group of people called Melungeons who were living here when the first settlers penetrated the area. Their origin has never been determined. Some have claimed the Bunches were part Melungeon, and this has infuriated Tyler. Perhaps for this reason he has been somewhat skeptical of outsiders, especially writers, and would never allow his picture to be taken. He told me that I was the first person that he ever allowed to photograph him. He laughs about the first time we met on a cold December afternoon when he was working in his tiny, improvised blacksmith shop.

I have bought numerous mountain relics from him over a twenty-five year period, but I had never asked about quilts. When I told Tyler and his wife that I was doing a book on quilts, to my surprise he told me of his experience as a quilter.

Tyler reminds me in many ways of Alex Stewart. They both live in Hancock County, seperated by only fifteen miles, but by a lot of rugged mountain terrain. They are both about as tough as men can be. They have been prodigious workers, they have mastered dozens of crafts and trades, and they are both gentle and compassionate men. Neither weighs one hundred pounds, "soaking wet." And the last thing I learned about both was that they could spin, weave, and make quilts. Many, and perhaps most men, would never have "lowered" themselves to do "women's" work, and if they did so, they wouldn't have admitted it. But both Alex and Tyler admitted to it, and were as proud of their ability to quilt as they were of their work as loggers, miners, trappers, etc. Tyler talked of his quilting, and of other aspects of his life.

Q. Well, Tyler I knew that you had worked at about every kind of work that there is, but I never knew you could quilt. Tell me about your quilting?

A. Up the creek here a little ways, up thar where I's born and raised, some old women was having a quilting. Well, I was standing there and one of them asked could I quilt — sorta as a joke. I told one of 'em to thread me up a needle. She got to laughin' and said 'You can't quilt!' And I said 'thread me a needle.' I took a piece of chalk and a string and made a fan, kinda you know. I made me out a round about six rows. I never seen no template. I quilted it and they ever one got up and looked at it. And they was *old* women. And ever one of 'em said 'He done a better job than ever one of us.' And said, 'You can just help finish this!' And I hoped (helped) 'em finish the whole quilt. (Tyler, at age 89 slapped his leg and laughed heartily at this recollection.) That was at Lewis Collins' down on the ridge, way back out there. That's been about seventy-five years ago.

Q. Where did you learn to quilt?

A. I learned myself — right at home. Momma died when I's 12 years old and they was seven little children and only one girl in the bunch and she was small. So that just left me and Pap to quilt of a night after we come in from working in the woods or in the corn field. I didn't make no patterns like people does now. I'd just get me some cloth and tear it in strips, maybe that wide, and as long as I wanted the quilt to be; and I'd change colors and sew them strips together.

Q. During your eighty-nine years you've worked at many different types of work, haven't you?

A. I worked at everthing a man could put his hands on. I'd go in and I'd say 'Have you got anything that you need done, and do ye need anyone to help you out?' I never would ask for no job, I knowed they's plenty of 'em. So I went to a place once, to a farmer, and ask 'Do you have any work you need to have done?' 'Plenty of it. What can you do?' I says, 'What do you want me to do?' He said, 'You're just too little to work. You can't do a man's work.' Men was a gettin' 50 cents a day for fifteen hours. Well, I says, 'I started out to work, and I'm gonna find it. If I can't get it here I can get it elsewhere.' I said, 'Being as I'm here, I'll help ye today, fer nothin. Then if you think I can do anything, I'll work some fer you.' I come in that night and I asked him, 'Well, what do you think about it?' And he said, 'Come back tomorrow.' I worked for that man six years straight. His name was John Russell and he lived over here at Hubbard Springs.

When I first started out I worked with the chain gang. Worked with them prisoners and them all dressed in stripes, and had 'em all tied to a big long chain with leg irons. I tamped ties for the railroads, and helped lay steel rails.

I worked up here in Virginia in the coke ovens for five our six years pulling coke. We'd burn that coal and make coke out of it, and it'd be so hot where you walked that sometimes it'd burn holes in our shoes. Have to pour water on your shoes to keep them from burning.

Q. Did you ever work in the coal mines?

A. Yeah, I opened two mines myself. I cased them up with timbers, and then I got me a buddy and we dug coal fer years. We didn't have no tracks, and it wasn't high enough for a mule, so we went back in that hole in under the mountain and dug it out with a pick, and then we'd roll it out on a wheelbarrow. He'd dig and I'd roll, then I'd dig and he'd roll it out. We'd take turn about thataway.

The mine was right in the woods just like right there. (Tyler pointed up toward the mountain that came to within a few feet of his front porch.) It was never cleared out and there was no road to it and me and that feller that was with me, we pulled that coal six miles over the mountain before we could get it out.

Q. The last time I was here, I guess it's been two years, you had just killed a big rattlesnake out there in front of your house.

A. Yeah, I rember that. He was a big un. I killed another un last year, and they's plenty more there now. It's time for them to crawl. This warm weather makes 'em crawl.

I told you about getting copperhead bit didn't I? Buddy, he really laid it to me! He hit me twice thar, 'fore I found out what it was. Pap was bare-footed, and had his britches legs rolled up to his knees, and hit was right after me. Pap jumped on it barefooted and stomped it to death. Hit was about as long as that, and I guess as big as that. (Tyler measures a yard with his outstretched hands, and compares its size to his arm.) He'd just pulled his shoes off and we'd started up to an old man's that lived up on top of the ridge. He had a big orchard of all kinds of fruit and we's goin' up thar to git some.

Every year when the snakes sheds (their skin) that place (where he was bitten) sheds just the same as a snake. Hit's done that ever year since it got well. I'd say that's been seventy-five year ago. My legs like to have rotted off from that. Didn't know nothin' to do fer it. Put a little turpentine on it and a hen egg to draw out the poison. We didn't have nothing to doctor or dentist with back then. (At this point Tyler rolls up the leg of his overall to show a discolored knot on the calf of his leg the size of a half embedded egg. Then he repeats.) That place will start hurting me and turning a different color, and then it'll shed off just about the same time the snakes start sheding their skins. Does that ever year.

"All I ever made was just old everyday quilts," Mrs. Bunch emphasized. "I never made no fancy quilts."

"Why I hate to say it, but I can quilt about as good as the old lady here," Tyler laughs.

FLOSSIE CORNETT
(Jeff, Kentucky)

In the very heart of the East Kentucky coal mining mountains, a few miles south of Hazard, is the village of Jeff. Bette Marshal, a native of the Kentucky mountains, who is now on the staff of Morehead College, had told me there were several quilters in that area, and that Flossie Cornett was a good example.

We found that Flossie was indeed a quilter and that she was most willing, and anxious, to discuss her favorite subject. She had a large quilt in a frame suspended from the ceiling in her living room, and was quilting on the March day we visited her. I asked her about her career as a quilter.

Q. Flossie, everywhere I look I see stacks of quilts you've made. I get the idea that you like to quilt?

A. Oh, Lord! I love it! I can set all day long and quilt. I love to set and quilt when it's snowing outside - just set there and quilt and watch the snow comin' down.

Q. Tell me about your childhood and how you got started quilting.

A. I was born down here at Little Leatherwood, Kentucky, about thirty somethin' miles from here. We was raised in a little log cabin that Daddy built hisself. We had it pretty rough but we never worried about nothin' to eat though. We raised it and we put it up. Everbody worked. We'd kill eight and nine big hogs ever fall. We'd have meat 'til that time next year. We had a big sixty-five gallon barrel of molasses. We had one full of pickled beans, one full of pickled corn, one full o' sulphured apples. We'd hole up (bury) apples, turnips, cabbage and potatoes and have them all winter. Even made our own vinegar from apple peeling. We didn't worry about where our meals come from. We had a cow. We had our milk and butter, and we had our chickens and our eggs.

We was raised in a Christian home. My daddy was a preacher. Started preachin' when I was 3 days old, and preached 'til he was 67. Had a stroke and had to quit. I started helping my mother quilt when I was 8 years old, and she died when I was 11. They was ten of us children and it took a lot of bed covers to keep warm. We tacked them — we didn't quilt them for the kids. Now, my mother made some nice quilts, but they was for company. My mother made nice quilts.

Q. And after you married, you continued to make quilts?

A. Oh, yeah. I was a Cornett and married a Cornett. I had eleven children and raised ten. They've all got their own homes. All but one has, and he's somewhere in Arizona. I'm so proud of them — every one.

Why, I've made eight or ten quilts lots of years. I've slowed down though as I've got older. Got down to four or five, and now I'm down to about three. I give them away to the children and grandchildren when they get married. I've got twenty-six grandchildren and I've made them baby quilts. I've made some that's so beautiful.

FLOSSIE CORNETT AND HER TOBACCO SACK QUILT

"The top of this quilt is made of Bull Durham tobacco sacks, and hit's as good as any material you can buy. My husband started working in the mines when he was 11 years old and he worked there 'til he got the black lung when he was 48 years old. He had all the miners who worked with him to save him them little tobacco sacks, and he'd bring them to me to make quilts. He was a good daddy."

ETHEL HALL

A few miles southeast of Hazard, Kentucky, in the village of Jeff, I saw an old gentleman working in his garden. Although it was in early February, he had turnips, spinach, lettuce, onions, and radishes already growing. He also had well-pruned grape vines and various types of fruit trees on his tiny lot of less than an acre. Anyone this industrious, I thought, would surely know the area, and would know where I might find some old-time quilters. Indeed he did know the region. He directed me to Boyd Hall's place which was located on the Left Fork of Mason's Creek a few miles up the hollow from the community of Viper, the home of Jean Richie, perhaps the country's best-known singer of old time mountain ballads.

I finally found the Left Fork of Mason's Creek, but had to make several inquiries to find the Boyd Hall homeplace. I was impressed by the warm, friendly manner in which I was greeted by every single person. The last place I stopped to ask directions was at a tiny country store. The woman operator volunteered to lock the store and go with me to the Halls', who happened to be her parents.

I found the old log house, now clothed with white weatherboarding, and I found 92 year old Boyd Hall supervising the spring plowing of his garden. He was also supervising a half dozen children who followed the turning plow, picking up red (earth) worms for fishing bait. Among those who were assisting in the bait gathering was Joanne, the youngest of his eighteen children.

Boyd was as affable and friendly as everyone else in that area. He said that if I was interested in quilts I'd have to see his wife Ethel. When Ethel came to the door she had a large butcher knife in her hand, holding it in such a manner as to cause some apprehension about her intent. My first impression was that she was going to the creek meadow below the house to get dry-land cresses, and other early plants for dinner, and this turned out to be the case.

I asked her about quilts, and before long we were in her tiny attic room or "hole" as Boyd called it. She had her quilting frame suspended from the ceiling, and around it there were four trunks, all filled with quilts, and piled high with other quilts which could not fit into the trunks. Most of the quilts were ones she had made, beautiful and colorful, and far superior to most of those of her contemporaries. She also had plain everyday quilts she had made strictly for use, and old quilts made by her grandmother. After we had taken several quilts to the porch and into the yard to be photographed, I asked this remarkable woman about her quilting, and about her life in the Kentucky mountains.

Q. Ethel, tell me about your early life; where you were born, where you grew up, and about your marriage.

A. I's raised here and yonder. Born across the mountains over around Wise, Virginia. I's a Cook (her family name) before I married. My daddy was a coal miner — had eight children and raised five of us. He'd go from one mine to another over in Virginia, and down here in Harlan.

Q. Well, tell me how you got started making quilts?

A. My grandmother made quilts. Just the old-timey tack quilts; just pieced up. Like the one I showed you out there a while ago. That's why I've kept her old quilts, you know, to show what she had done back in her days.

My mother would make a quilt ever now and then; old everday quilts. But mostly Grandma would make quilts for my mother to use. Her name was Sarah Jane Cook. She was a Breeden before she married.

I never quilted much til after I married Boyd here. He'd been married before and had five little children when I married him and one dead. We started having children of our own; so we had to have a lot of bed cover, and that's when I really started quilting. I had twelve children of my own.

Back then we didn't have none of this here 'lectricity, and we didn't have no sich thing as 'lectric blankets. You just had to pile quilts on to keep warm in the winter. Law, when I come here this was just an old log house! Had three rooms, is all they was, and a loft.

Me and Jim, one of the older boys, we went out in the woods and cut timber ourselves, and hauled the logs to the saw mill and got the lumber sawed. Then we'd pile the rough lumber here in front of the fire place, and we'd dress it down with them old hand planes of a night. We ceiled over the old rough logs, and we weather-boarded the outside, and painted it white.

Then we added on the new kitchen there, and that back room, and we added that porch on the front and side, and the back porch too. But we didn't have nothin' like a living room back when I come here. Just the kitchen and these two rooms. We'd put the boys in one bed, sometimes four or five, and the girls in the other.

Q. The first quilts you made — I suppose they were not the pretty, fancy quilts like you make now?

A. Oh, no. I first started out on the tack quilts. Piecin' up from old overhalls (overalls). He (Boyd) wore old overhalls all the time then. I'd use any good pieces from them overhalls after he'd wore them out, and pieces of old coats and things people would give us.

They had a clothing sale up here at Blackley, at Robinson school, and we'd go up there and buy bundles of clothes. Twenty-five cent bundles, and I'd take stuff outta that and cut them old clothes up and make clothes for all the children. We didn't have no money to by no cloth.

Q. What kind of work has Boyd followed?

A. Well, he worked on WPA, in the coal mines a few years, and he worked around fer people, you know, and buildin' these roads, and he had an old horse and he'd plow for people to buy us a little somethin' to eat, and to buy feed for the horse. They'd pay him so much a day. We had a hard time livin'.

While he was workin' off, me and the kids would farm. Yeah, we raised our own corn, made our own meal. I had an old cow too, and we took and raised feed fer her. Fodder; we'd save our fodder. We raised our potatoes, beans, corn, stuff like that, you know. I had my chickens you know, and we got eggs. Raised cane and made our molasses. Butter and molasses tasted purdy good to me then. We didn't have nothing fancy like hamburgers and hotdogs and stuff like that.

Q. What did you do with the little children, the babies, while you were out working in the fields.?

A. Well, we had a bigger one (child) to stay here and take care of my little children. I tell ye, I'd go out and leave my babies and they would be two weeks old. I'd go out in the field and leave my little babies, and they'd feed 'em you know, a little milk an' stuff. I'd come in and let the little fellers nurse — they nursed the breast.

Buddy, I've worked like a man. Spring o' the year come I used to put on my overalls and tie my head up and put me on a coat, and go back there in that field with my mattock and go back there and grub, from daylight til dark and snow just a flyin'. I tell ye we had to make our own livin' and raise our family.

Q. When you say "grubbing" you're talking about digging out the young tree sprouts. Many people wouldn't know what grubbing is today, would they?

A. No, not many people knows what it is today — they wouldn't know hardly what kind of a tool you'd use to grub with. I used a mattock and an ax, or just anything to get that sprout out of the ground. Work all day long. Come in just long enough to get a little snack then take off — back to grubbin'. You had to go way down in the ground and get all the roots or it'd come back on you.

Q. I don't suppose that you had a mowing machine?

A. We didn't have no sich a thing in them days. Didn't have no money to buy one, and if we did have, the mountainside was too steep to get on. If you cut a sprout off it just keeps coming back ever year, and you just have to go on cutting it. But once you dig it out by the roots, then you're through with it.

Q. In addition to your five step-children, you had twelve of your own. How were you able to provide medicine and pay the doctor bills?

A. We made our own — what we had. There's certain kinds of tea that's good for certain diseases. I made spicewood tea, sassafras tea, and I've made peppermint tea and catnip tea. I used wild cherry tree bark for tonic and to build up our blood. We used slip elm bark to chew for a laxative. For worms for our children we'd take molasses and boil 'em down and put this worm pepper seed in 'em. I bet you know what that is. It growed wild and we'd go gather it. It's got a kind of a peculiar taste to it, and it'll shore bring the worms.

Q. Did you go to the hospital when your children were born?

A. Never had a child in a hospital in my life. I had a doctor three times with my children, but the rest of them were with mid-wives. They called them granny women.

They didn't charge hardly anything, but you pay dear now if you go to the hospital. Most of my babies was delivered by Granny Hettie Caudle, and another old lady called Granny Mart Caudle. Now them two delivered a lot of babies. They just lived right over here on the top of the mountain about three miles. They's some akin to each other, but I don't know how much.

Boyd'd have to go get them, sometimes in the middle of the night. Sometimes he'd go on the old horse, and sometimes he'd walk. They'd stay with you all day and all night if they had to, and sometimes longer. And they'd charge about $5.00. My first babies was twins — twin girls. And it was five years then 'fore I had another baby. He was my oldest boy. I had one boy killed in a car wreck in 1955. He'd been in the Army and he'd just come back home — I think about twelve days.

Back then you couldn't even get a horse and buggy up this hollow. Doc Combs, old Doctor Combs, we used to have him once in a while when the children were bad sick. He had a big fat horse, and he'd unhitch him from the buggy and come up here a few times.

Q. Well, we've talked about how you first made quilts soon after you married, and we've talked about your farming and outside work. We haven't talked much about your quilting in recent years.

A. I'd quilt mostly in the winter time cause in the summertime I had to get out and make somethin' to eat. In a winter I've made as high as eight or ten quilts. Piece them by the piece or piece them in fans. I'd put all the pieces together of a night by the fire, and then the next day when I could see, I'd do the quilting.

I's 18 when I married, and I've been quilting ever since. Ever winter. That's my hobby. Ever winter I set right upstairs there and make my quilts.

Q. You must have given many of your quilts away?

A. Lord yeah! Ever Christmas that's their Christmas presnet and their birthday presents, or somethin' er nother like that. I've got a girl in Indiana and she ain't got a quilt in her house but what I hadn't made her. I've give that one over there (she points to her youngest daughter, Joanne) two or three. I made her an awful purdy onc and give her a brand new one for my grandbaby. I've made my grandchildren quilts and give 'em.

Q. Well, they'll appreciate them someday a lot more than they do now.

A. Well some of them say they're gonna put them in their hope chest and keep them to remember Mamaw by. They call me Mamaw. My grandchildren are just as great to me as my children. I love 'em just as good.

Q. Down in Tennessee most of the old people raised a little cotton, but they had to plant it very early, and even then it hardly matured before frost. I was wondering if cotton could be raised this far north - to use as batting for quilts?

A. My grandmother, when she gardened, I can remember her planting it and raising it. She used to live up the holler up here that they call Ben Davis Holler. She raised just a little cotton; just bunches here and yonder. I tell you what she did do. When she's a livin', ever fall, you've seed these milkweeds ain't you? You know what they are. That stuff that busts out and looks like feathers. She'd take her a big sack, and when them busted out she'd go gather enough of that to make her fillings with.

(This was a most interesting and revealing bit of information, which I had never heard before, but this fluffy, silk-like substance, similar to fine down, would likely work extremely well for this purpose.)

Q. What else was used for the padding?

A. What we used most in them days for padding was the linings out of old coats. You know they've got a quiltin' in them. Put them together and make paddin' fer them quilts. Or either we'd take old wore-out quilts, and put them in there and make paddin' outta them. If you have a old wore-out blanket you could use that. Now them that you saw out there, they're mostly padded with old wore-out blankets. Except that one that my grandmother made, and I think she padded hit with old wore-out shirts and things like that. Made it at Hazard. Laid it on a bed and tacked it. That's the way I tack all my quilts — lay them on a bed and tack them out.

I don't quilt with a thimble. You know what I make a thimble out of? These old overhall cloth. You outta see my thimble. I'm scared to death when I get a thimble on my finger! I sure am. I don't know, seems like I'm afraid that needle will slip out and hit me in the hand, you know. I take that cloth thimble, and buddy that needle don't slip! It'll go through that sometimes though. Right here's what I quilt with (shows me the thimble made out of old overalls.) See right here now where that needles went in that thick part.

Q. Did you ever see anybody else do that?

A. No, just picked it up myself. I just knowed I had to have a thimble of some kind to protect my fingers. And I made that. I've done that all my life, quilting like that. Now my children quilt with a thimble.

Q. I talked with a woman the other day that stood up all the time while she quilted.

A. Well, I stand up a whole lot. I get tired of settin', and I get up and stretch my legs. See, I've had a stroke back about two year ago, and hit hurts me to sit so long. After I sit so long my legs, my left side, gets numb.

Q. How many hours a day do you quilt?

A. I go up there ever mornin' after I clean my house up. I go upstairs. I come downstairs about 1 or 2 o'clock and cook somethin' to eat. We eat and I wash my dishes up and go back upstairs and stay 'til about 4:30 and come down and do up the work.

Q. Don't you ever get tired and lonesome setting up there all day in that little room by yourself, quilting?

A. No! I never get tired, I just love to quilt. I'd druther quilt than eat on the hungriest day ever I seen.

Ethel Hall, of the Left Fork of Mason's Creek, near Viper in the east Kentucky mountains, is shown here during the author's interview with her in February, 1983.

Ethel Hall, left, and her daughter Joanne hold an overall tack quilt made by Ethel's grandmother.

The back of the overall quilt is made from fertilizer sacks which apparently originated in Argentina.

Ninety-two year old Boyd Hall with his wife Ethel, and Joanne, the youngest of his eighteen children, and the youngest of Ethel's twelve children.

"When I married Boyd and came here when I's 18 years old, this was jist a little log cabin. Me and the boys went to the woods, cut the timber, sawed it and added these rooms and porches," Ethel states. She is shown here sunning a few of her quilts.

DOLPHIA ELKINS OF NEW LOYSTON
(Seventy-two years a quilter)

Dolphia George Elkins lives in a peaceful and pastoral valley at the edge of the village of New Loyston, some twenty miles north of Knoxville. Her house is an early hand-hewn log one, though it's now covered inside and out so that one would never suspect its pioneer vintage. Dolphia has been living in the comfortable old home since she married Charlie Elkins in 1921.

Her mother Ida George was a quilter, and some of her quilts are included elsewhere in this book. Dolphia helped her mother quilt as a girl, and made some everyday quilts in the first years of her marriage. She helped operate the dairy farm, raised a garden each year, helped her husband operate his country store for half a century, and raised four children. She was not active as a quilter during these years, but in 1964 the children were grown, the farming chores and management had largely been assumed by others, and Dolphia again took up quilting. She has made dozens since that time.

She talked about how quilting had changed through the years.

Back then when I was first married we just used anything we could get to make quilts out of. Take men's clothes and cut the best out of them you know. They call them comforts — they're tacked in. Well they wasn't no pattern to them, just sew them in strips. They's awful thick — where they was made out of thick material. They'd tack them, and just called 'em comforts. They's heavy too. But them old heavy wool quilts felt good then, on a cold night.

This house wasn't like it is now. It was open and had an ole chimney at the other end of that kitchen and it was open and I tell you we like to froze to death. That was in 1939. Law me, you raise three boys and a girl, and me and Charlie, we used a whole lot of quilts back then. That was the only cover we had. We'd have five or six quilts on every bed.

But now we use all the pretty patterns. The quilts are not made so much for warmth as they are to look pretty. I make three or four every winter; but some winters I wouldn't make but two.

Quilting is enjoyable, and it helps to pass off the time. Yeah. Yeah, I've been wanting to put me up another quilt, but then I think it's too big a job for me. But I like to quilt.

Dolphia George Elkins, like tens of thousands of quilters from across the country, has numerous quilt tops packed away in her upstairs trunks and quilt chests.

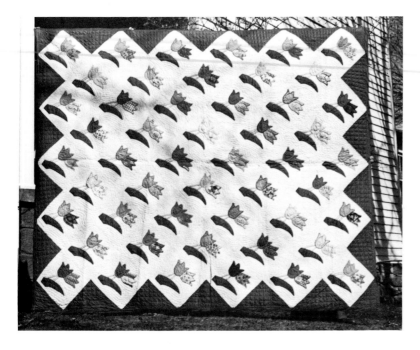

This intricately stitched Tulip quilt is one of many Dolphia Elkins has made and carefully packed away.

The quilt shown here at Dolphia Elkins' home is one she has had packed away in the upstairs cedar chest since she made it several years ago.

PAULINE LAY OF
WHITE COUNTY, TENNESSEE
(with quilt made by her great-great grandmother)

Pauline Brown Lay, like several generations of her ancestors, is a native of White County in Middle Tennessee. Her interest and affinity for quilts is perhaps traceable to the encounters she had as a child with her grandmother, her great-grandmother, and their quilts.

She is shown here with the Four-Pointed Star quilt made by her great-great-grandmother Marge Brown of the Doyle Community in White County, Tennessee. Pauline talked about this tattered quilt with feeling and affection. "My daddy always liked that quilt and claimed it, but his grandmother never gave it to him. She was part Indian — sort of a funny lady. Anyway, it was claimed by Daddy, and they all knew it, and when his grandmother died they gave the quilt to him. She had used it fifty years, I guess — but after Daddy got it, him and Mother only used it occasionally. They didn't want to wear it out because Daddy thought so much of it. He had dreamed about having that quilt since he slept under it as a child."

When her niece, Chris Keys, brought Pauline by the Museum recently, I plied her with questions about quilts, and her quiet and reticent personality turned to one of enthusiasm.

Oh, I do like to quilt! My mother started quilting when she was a young girl and she quilted sixty years, I guess. My grandmother before her quilted; and I would say she quilted seventy years.

I don't just set down and quilt all day long, I quilt between times — when I don't have anything else to do. I quilt a lot at night while my husband watches T.V., and he says: 'What do you want to make more quilts for? You've got more quilts now than you'll ever use.' And I say, 'Well, I can sit here and quilt and when spring comes I've got something to show for what I've done, and you don't have one thing.'

THE MARTIN SISTERS OF
PANTHER CREEK

I don't know how many chests and trunks full of quilts there are in the large Martin farmhouse, a few miles above Sneedville, Tennessee. I have visited with the three Martin sisters often over a period of many years, and while they were most friendly and jovial, they were never wont to show off their antiques and household relics.

It was almost dark when Robin and I stopped there on the way home from a day with Alex Stewart. I asked Ila Mae if they had any old quilts, and she laughed heartily at the question. "Why, son, they's trunks and chests full of 'em; but you know how Maude is. She's quare — she probably won't let you get them out."

Indeed, Maude was reluctant, but finally agreed to open a large chest which sat near the fireplace in the living room. She barely opened the lid, but enough for us to see that it was filled with what appeared to be old and unused quilts. Not only did we not get into any of the bedrooms, nor any of the upstairs rooms, we didn't get beyond the top quilt in this one chest. Maude pulled the first quilt out, then quickly closed the lid. So we may all wonder how many fine old quilts there are packed away in the rambling white house on Panther Creek.

Sisters Maude Martin, left, and Ila Mae are shown here in front of the old homeplace holding one of the many quilts made by their mother and grandmother.

Maude Martin, left, and her sister Nit never married and have spent their lives at the old homeplace. "In the spring time," Maude said, "we have a job sunning all them quilts and coverlets." (Photograph by the author)

Maude, who is 83 and who "puts in a day's work every day" is holding the quilt which her mother made. (Photograph by the author)

LILLIAN STINER—SEVENTY-SIX YEARS A QUILTER

When I called 88-year-old Lillian Stiner about visiting with her in her Knox County, Tennessee, home, she was cordial, friendly and eager to talk about quilting. However, she informed me she would soon be leaving to see her youngest great-grandchild in Florida, and apologized for having only limited time.

When I got to her modern brick home in Halls Cross Roads, I found her luggage piled by the garage door. I found also a spry, agile and gracious lady who, in all aspects of appearance, looked like a woman twenty years her junior.

It was difficult to talk because of the telephone interruptions. Her granddaughter wanted advice on how to cook pithy turnips, neighbors called to say goodbye, and finally a special phone call—from her boyfriend. It was 96 year old Harvey Loy and I could hear and recognize his booming voice from where I sat, ten feet away from the phone. After her conversation with Harvey, I commented on his youthfulness and the fact that he was so active. "Oh, yeah," Lillian said. "He drove over here last night and took me out to eat. He drove all the way across Knoxville to the place where we ate. But he's getting to where he doesn't like to drive on the interstate here in town at night too much."

Lillian's father was Dr. Winfield Scott Davis of Big Valley in Union County, Tennessee, the area where my ancestors also settled in the late 1700's when that region was an isolated wilderness. I asked her about her life in the beautiful and historic valley, and about her long career as a quilter.

> Oh, I love to make quilts. I was just a little girl when I started — when my mother taught me. I was maybe 12 or 13 years old. I made, or helped make, quilts on until I was married. Then after I was married I started making quilts for our use, and later to give away. I was married almost fifty years and I quilted all that time. Then about twenty years ago, after my husband died, I started quilting for the church.
>
> A group of elderly ladies, and some not so elderly, would quilt for people that had quilt tops that had never been quilted. We'd charge them so much, then we'd give all the money to the church, Halls Central Methodist. We were doing it for the church, and for the people too; for two purposes. They were tickled to death to get their quilts quilted, and they paid us a fair price to get them done.

A youthful 88-year-old Lillian Stiner with two of the quilts she made and didn't give away.

When I was helping to make the quilts at home we just made plain quilts because of the warmth, and because we needed them to sleep under. We didn't make fancy quilts, although we had some very fancy quilts that had been made by my grandmothers. It seems to go in cycles. They made some fancy quilts back then in my grandparents time; then they got to making just plain ones. And now, in a lot of places, they're back to the fancy ones again.

Not counting the years that I quilted for the church, I've made, with the help of my daughters, about a hundred twenty-five, I guess. Never did sell one. Gave them away to my grandchildren, and of course we wore a lot of them out, raising six children, you know.

We quilted the year 'round. Of course more quilting was done in the winter time, when it was too cold and bad to get out and do anything else. But we quilted in the summer, too. Me and my children would go out under the shade trees in the yard and quilt. Take the quilting frames out there and quilt. We just loved to do it. Oh, they didn't like it as well as I did, but they helped me anyway. They were very good hands to do it. My daughter still makes them. She makes lovely quilts. Her name is Ann; Ann Schultz.

I asked Lillian to tell me a little about her early life.

Well as you know, my father was a country doctor. Had his little doctor's office right there next to the house where we lived. He was a school teacher, then he went to school and became a doctor and practiced over fifty years. He traveled all over Union County and part of Claiborne County on horseback and in a buggy. Sometimes I'd go with him when he was going to see somebody we knew.

I started teaching when I was 18 years old. I taught at the one-room school at Irwin's Chapel, and my salary was $40.00 a month. Then I was assistant to my husband after I was married, and I just made $35.00 a month. Then I taught in a two-room school with Mr. (Harvey) Loy. He was the principal and I was his assistant. That was at what they called Union School in Union County, and the pay was just $30.00 a month.

That was in 1914. Let's see, that's been—this is '83—that's been sixty-nine years ago. There were ninety-eight students in the school, and he and I made a hundred in the group. I had forty-eight students in my room and he had fifty. Back then we worked at it! (Laughter)

Oh, yes I like to make quilts; but I've about quit. Some of the women who were in the quilting group at the church died, some are sick and disabled, and some are just too old—like me (laughter). Oh, I can quilt, but I've retired from all the fancy work. I help my daughter quilt on hers.

Lillian and Harvey are shown here with their students at Union School in Union County, Tennessee, sixty-nine years ago, in 1914. Lillian is at the extreme left and Harvey is at the far right. He was the principal of the school, and had fifty students; and she was his assistant, with forty-eight scholars.

Lillian is shown here with Harvey Loy, her 96 year old friend who frequently drives her across Knoxville to their favorite restaurant.

HANNAH LANE
FROM COAL MINING TO QUILT MAKING

Hannah Lane lives in the beautiful hills of extreme southwestern Virginia, about halfway between the two historic little towns of Gate City and Fort Blackmore. Maybe that's why the community is called Midway. I had known Hannah for some time, but had no idea whether or not she was a quilter. But, since Robin and I were passing through the area, we decided to stop. One question about quilting was all that was necessary to encourage Hannah to tell us all about her longtime interest in making quilts.

She took us through the back rooms where several dozen quilts were piled on the beds, in chairs and in every available space. All of these she had made over half a century as a quilter. In addition to the completed quilts, there were many other quilt tops stored in trunks and in boxes, waiting their turn to be quilted. Hannah was so interested in showing us her handiwork and in discussing her love for quilts that I had a difficult time getting her back to the kitchen table where I had placed my recorder for the purpose of interviewing her.

It was during the interview that Hannah casually mentioned her experiences as a coal miner. From digging coal to piecing quilts, I thought, had to be the most extreme occupational variation yet found in a quilter. Hannah was just as proud of her days as a coal miner as she was as a quilter.

Q. Hannah, you said you started helping your mother quilt when you were very young. Tell me about your early childhood and your early quilting.

A. Well, I started helping my mother make quilts before I was old enough to go to school. I could sew pieces together when I don't guess I's over 5 years old. I wasn't big enough to quilt but I'd help her piece. They was eleven children in my mother's family — eight boys and three girls, and so it took a heap of quilts to do a family that size.

Q. I believe you told me that you were born near Pikeville, Kentucky. That's a coal mining area. Was your father a miner?

A. He had a little land, and we farmed and we dug coal for our own use. The boys - one of them went to the first World War and the other married and left home - and I was the boy from then on out. I'd go with him (her father) to the coal bank (mine) and help him dig coal. He was gettin' on up in years. He'd bore the holes and put the powder and the dynamite and everything in, and get out to where he could see daylight. I would strike the match to light it with and set it off. There was one bank where we lived before he bought this place, and they was a track back in there and they had a buggy. But most of the mines — they'd never been no track put in them. We had to shovel the coal out to the mouth.

Q. You'd have to shovel several times, wouldn't you?

A. Oh, quite a few! Back then I could throw a shovel full o' coal then plum from here to the far end of this house.

Q. And then you'd have to get it and shovel it again; a few more feet toward the entrance?

A. Yessir, several times until we got it out of the mouth of the bank. When we lived at the head of Ferguson's Creek, we worked in a mine for a while that had a little wooden track and what they called a buggy where we could push the coal out by hand on that buggy, and not have to throw it out by shovel. Oh, we thought that was the greatest thing that ever was. Oh, I'd love to go back up there so bad, I just can't hardly stand it. It's been years and years since I's back up there. I've dug many a lump of coal up there at the head of Ferguson's Creek — in them mountains. I stayed home til I was 17 and helped my daddy farm and dig coal. He was getting old and disabled and couldn't do much.

Q. Now, when you say dug it, did you dig it with a pick?

A. Yes sir. After it was shot down, we'd get that out of the way. It was easy dug you know, it being loose. Then when we'd get that dug down, we wouldn't dig anymore until he'd bore more holes and shoot out more coal.

We had what we called a coal lamp. It was a little round lamp, about that big and about that deep. The wick come straight up the middle and the wick — well it was just about as big as your little finger, I guess. It burned what we called lamp oil. People call it kerosene now — but we called it just plain ole lamp oil. I can remember when my mother didn't have matches! Now I don't know if there was any matches anywhere else or not, but if they was, we didn't have 'em. I've seen her take two pieces of flint and rub 'em together and have a piece of cotton, and that was the way we got our fire. Made our own fires.

Q. Well, Hannah, tell me about your quilting.

A. I loved it. And I love it yet, if I just had room and could. But my hands has been real bad. That's the reason I ain't got these quilts quilted.

Q. You said you were 76. You don't look that old.

A. Well, I feel like I'm 176 sometimes. I started helping my mother piece quilts. She would piece these Eight Points on paper, and tear the paper off then.

Q. How many quilts have you made over the years?

A. Mercy goodness, Brother! I never did keep account of 'em. I've sold quite a few and I've give the younguns — I give 'em all one apiece this Christmas and about five years ago I give 'em one apiece at Christmas.

Q. You say you enjoy quilting when you don't have anything else to do?

A. Why if I had anything else to do and could leave it, I'd leave it and quilt. I just love to quilt. I love to crochet and I love to piece quilts. I'd druther sit down and piece one as to quilt it. But I do love to quilt.

Hannah Lane, whose childhood was divided between making quilts and mining coal, is shown here with one of her unfinished quilt tops. It is one of many she had pieced, but not quilted.

MARTHA TURNER OF GENESIS ROAD

Eighty-four-year-old Martha Turner's life today bears little resemblance to that she knew as a child on the Cumberland Mountain plateau near Crossville, Tennessee. Though she still lives on Genesis Road in the rural Oak Hill Community near her ancestral home, she has electricity, a telephone, television and other modern conveniences. There is nothing in her present day "front" room to remind her of the primitive home of her childhood—except the old quilting frame.

I must say this residual of the past appears to be a little incongruous in the modern setting; but it was a most practical device then, and it remains so today. When Martha feels like quilting, she merely lowers the frame, raising it when she is finished.

I asked Martha how long she had been quilting, and what she did with all the quilts she made. I asked about her family, and her life on the Cumberland Plateau.

Oh, it's been so long back that I don't remember when I started quilting. I've lived here for fifty-six years, and I was quilting before that. We had eight children and just twenty acres of land; so we all had to work. My husband died in 1953, and I had all the children to raise. I plowed in the fields with the mules, and I've done ever kind of work a man did. I made a big garden til year before last. My rheumatism got so bad in my knees that I had to give up all that kind of work; but I still quilt. I guess I made fifteen or twenty a year, and I give them all away. I give them for Christmas presents, to my children, grandchildren and great-grandchildren. This one here is for my youngest daughter Joyce.

Martha Turner, as we found her on a cold winter day January, 1983, at her suspended frame quilting as she has done for most of her 84 years.

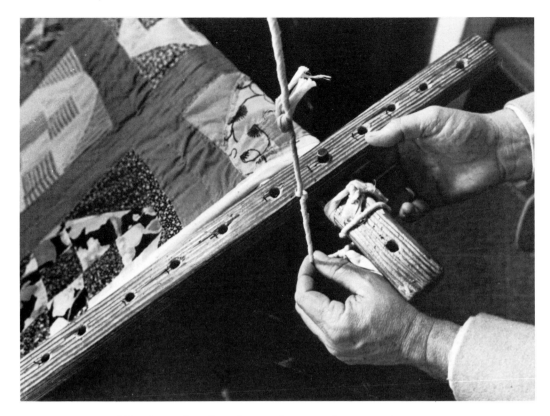

Martha raises her frame by merely wrapping
the cloth cord around one section of the frame.

Once the frame is raised, the room is
returned to normal.

WILLIE'S CHURCH QUILTS

Willie Stooksbury Irwin spent several years caring for her invalid father and for her husband, Morrell Irwin whose last years were inactive because of a heart condition. After their respective deaths she discovered several bags of quilt scraps her mother Kate Stooksbury had saved over the years, and some that may have been stored away by her grandmother Ida George. Many of these scraps had been given to her mother by neighbors who knew of her fondness for making quilts. Much of the material was from chicken and cow feed sacks, and some of the material saved for the quilt backs was from flour and fertilize sacks. Along with these quilt scraps there were also a number of large bags filled with cotton she had grown, seeded and stored away for the batting.

Although Willie had had only limited exposure to quilting as a girl, she decided to "work up" some of the pieces left by her mother, and to her surprise, she found quilting to be a fascinating pastime. She has made over eight quilts from the scraps her mother had, and there are enough left for several more. She has ample cotton left for the padding.

The quilts are of good quality, all hand-pieced and quilted. Her price is $40.00 each. It is not surprising that one of her neighbors bought her entire supply the day after this photograph was made. All the proceeds from the quilts go to the church. So, like many quilters, her enjoyment comes, not from monetary considerations, but from the self-satisfaction of creating a beautiful object.

116

ALEX STEWART, THE QUILTER AT 92

The fabulous Alex Stewart has mastered literally dozens of crafts, professions, and avocations. After visiting with him for almost a quarter century, I thought I knew them all. He is a master blacksmith, musical instrument maker, miller, netmaker, stone mason, carpenter, herb doctor, well-digger, chair maker, trapper, tanner, moonshiner, cross bow maker, beekeeper, cook, folk art carver and is doubtless the nation's best known old-time cooper. I am familiar with these and scores of other skills he possesses. I knew also that he could knit, spin, card and weave, but I had no idea that this venerable old gentleman from Panther Creek, in Hancock County, Tennessee, could also quilt.

We were attending his 92nd birthday party, in January 1983, when the idea occurred of photographing him holding one of the quilts his late wife had made. The house was full of dozens of well-wishers, and I got his daughter Edith to go into the back room with me to select a quilt. When we handed it to Alex to hold I jokingly asked if he could quilt.

The quilt Alex Stewart is holding was the last one made by his wife Margie who died several years ago, ending their marriage of over sixty-five years. While this is a colorful quilt, most of those he had were of the old utilitarian patchwork type made from scraps of old coats and woolen trousers.

"You get me a needle and thread and I'll show you whether I can quilt or not," he laughed confidently. Well, Edith did get the needle and thread and as she did so she said, "I'll tell you right now that Pap can quilt — better than a lot of women, I guess." Sure enough, he grabbed the needle like an expert and started sewing and talking at the same time, to the amusement of all the women who were watching.

Unlike some men who can sew and do other "women's" work, Alex was not the least bit hesitant to admit it. On the contrary, he was proud of these skills, and he often bragged about his spinning, knitting and weaving.

I asked Alex a few questions about quilt related subjects.

Q. Alex, tell me about your involvement with quilt making.

A. Oh, I've helped make many a quilt. I've carded a many batten to put in quilts. I used to set down and card for Mommy and she'd have her frames up and her lining in and I'd set there and card that batten and she'd put 'em in. I could card rolls to spin just as good as she could, but she was a hand at that. But, I could spin as good as a woman.

Q. Did she make a lot of quilts?

A. Oh, yeah, that's the biggest thing she done. Boy, she was the best hand to quilt I ever saw in my life. I've never saw nobody yet that could beat her.

Q. What did they use for the filler? Was it mostly cotton or wool?

A. Well, now just say you had some blankets or old quilts that was gettin' old and ragged. She'd put that in between instead of batten. But she used cotton more'n anything. They's two pounds of cotton in ever quilt she quilted. Two pound of cotton will mean more than a feller thinks it will. She'd spin it and make the thread to weave the cloth — weave her lining. Then (she would) have to spin the thread to do the quilting with.

Q. The back of it would be hand spun?

A. Yeah, ever bit of it.

Q. And then what about the top, how would it be made?

A. Oh, she'd quilt hit outta little pieces; make it purdy, you know. Like I's tellin' you a while ago. I've made her many designs on the quilt top for her to quilt by. Oh, I'd make different kinds of designs on them for her. They'd be three squares in there that were just a foot apart, then I'd take a big plate and set down and take a piece of cloth thataway, and then go around it. Then set a compass right in the center of that and make flowers in there.

Sometimes it would take her a month to quilt a quilt. She didn't pay no attention to that. She'd just work ever minute she had to spare. She'd make, sometimes, a wreath and put a strip up here thataway. And they was purdy. Turn that up towards the head of the bed and it made the bed look good. I'd make some of the patterns for her.

Q. Where did you learn to make these patterns?

A. Well, I learned the most of it from my Grandpap. I just watched him how he done it and I done the rest of it myself. She'd quilt pieces, I'll swear you would not believe it. She'd quilt the squares that wouldn't be much bigger'n that right there. (Alex measures off a quarter inch length with his thumb and finger.) Yeah, I ferget how many — she knowed how many it took — it took a thousand an somethin' er nother. And, she'd have them different colors, and she'd take and put different colors in there and make it purdy.

People back then saved ever rag they got. They'd use it fer something or nother — dishrag, quilt patches, or something. Lord, I've seen clothes that you couldn't tell what it was made out of for the patches. I've wore lots of them sort of like that; but not quite that bad.

Q. Did they use wool for the inside of the quilt?

A. They would when they's makin' comforts. What they call comforts. That's just as heavy again as a ordinary quilt. But, they'd put wool in that. Sometimes they'd used old cloths and rags; tear them up and make filling out of them.

Q. Did you use the suspended, or ceiling, frames?

A. That's the first quiltin' ever I saw done. My Grandma Livesay — that was my mother's mother — she got uncle Newt Livesay to make her some quiltin' hosses. And Mommy would go down there and help her quilt. I was with her down there and she talked to her and she said, 'I'd shore like to have that (the quilting hosses) that's so handy.' She said, 'You can roll or set that over against the wall or anywhere you want to out of your way.' I said, 'Well, I'll make ye a pair.' She said, 'Why, you can't.' I said, 'I know I can!' I went out and got the timber and made her a pair. Like to have tickled her to death.

Q. What kind of bed covers did the real poor people have on Newman's Ridge when you were growing up?

A. Why, they's two-thirds of the people didn't know nothin' about quiltin'. Didn't have quilts. Just old shucks, leaves, rags and thangs. Never had a quilt in the house.

Q. Well, old quilts are bringing good prices these days.

A. Yeah, they's two women come here, ain't been too long ago, that I'd never seed before nor heered tell of. They's the slouchy-est lookin' women, in a way, that ever I seen. They was clean, but they was slouchy dressed and everthing. Great long dresses they's wearing. And they come up here and spoke to me and asked me if I had any old timey quilts I'd sell. I said, 'No, don't guess I have.'

'Well, now', she said, 'You've got some I guess and just won't sell 'em'. She said, 'Well, do you mind me seein' some of 'em?' I said, 'No, I don't care for you a lookin' at some.' She went in there (in his bedroom) and she was just into everthing. I had a trunk a settin' there and the said, 'How many you got in that trunk?' Well, I said, 'I guess it's full.' She wanted me to get them out and show them to her and I wouldn't do it. Oh, she just begged me to. She said, 'I'll just give you what you ask for 'em' — for the one I had layin' in there on the bed. Ask me who quilted it. I said, 'No! Mommy quilted that for me,' and I said, 'And money won't buy it.' Well she said she thought maybe she could get one or two off of me, but I said, 'No, they's all made by my mother and my wife, and I ain't got none for sale.'

OPAL HARNESS HATMAKER—SIXTY YEARS A QUILTER

When Opal Hatmaker was 5 years old her coal mining father, Jerry Harness, died leaving her mother with thirteen children, and a fourteenth child born three months later. Their home was in a remote mining section of Anderson County, Tennessee, in a community called Laurel Grove. There was no social security then, no death benefits and no insurance. Mrs. Harness employed all her resourcefulness and ingenuity in an endeavor to sustain her large family. Quilting became the mainstay. Even though Opal was only 5 at the time, she remembers well how it was.

Pap died February 10, 1918. He worked in the mines down in Briceville in the old Tennessee Holler, I believe. That's the last work that I remember that he did.

Q. Well, that was about eight or ten miles from where you lived in Laurel Grove. How did he get to work?

A. He walked back and forth. He said he went to the mines many a morning with his britches legs froze. Said he worked in water in the mines many times, and when he'd walk home of a night, in the winter, his britches would freeze stiff and he couldn't walk.

Q. Walking the sixteen miles was almost a days work. How many hours a day did he work in the coal mine down there? Ten hours or more?

A. Oh, yes. Maybe longer. I remember him a leavin' long before daylight and gettin' in after dark. Mother said he worked in the water, and gettin' out in the cold walking home was what caused him to take that flu and die. That was in the big flu epidemic when so many people died.

Q. You've told me that your mother depended on quilting, to a great extent, to feed the family. I suppose you helped?

A. (She laughed heartily) I reckon I did! I started tacking quilts, they call it tying now, when I was 7 or 8 years old. And if us girls didn't do it right, she'd make us take it out and do it again. That's why I learned it.

Q. Your mother made quilts to sell?

A. She made 'em to sell, and then a lot of people would bring us the material and we would make the quilts for them. Then, of course, it took a lot of quilts to keep that

many kids warm. They's so many of us that we had to use anything we could get in order to have enough cover. You didn't see nothing like a blanket or anything back in them days.

Q. The quilts you made for yourself, would they be patchwork quilts with various patterns?

A. Naw, we just made them out of old heavy clothing. They'd be too tough to quilt. We'd just take a big darning needle and run through them and tie them. We called them tack quilts. They didn't have no pattern, ner no quilting. They was just made out of big pieces of old wore-out coats, pants and so forth. And we'd use feed sacks, and flour sacks.

Q. Did you use cotton for the filling?

A. No. We just stuffed them with any old rags that couldn't be used for anything else. We raised a little cotton but not enough for quilt lining. My mother made socks and gloves and things out of what little cotton we raised. She had a spinning wheel where she'd make her thread.

Q. Those kind of "quilts" I've always heard called comforters.

A. We just called them tack quilts. (She laughs) It didn't take long to make a tack quilt. We'd all get around and tack one out in about two or three hours.

Q. When did the family do most of the quilting?

A. All the time when it was too cold or rainy to work outside in the fields or gardens. We never wasted no time (she chuckles). When it was too wet to work outside, she had us working inside. All the girls worked on quilts.

Q. What about the boys?

A. They used to help tack 'em. Yeah, they'd help sew, but they was embarrassed if somebody come in and saw it. (Much laughter) They thought that was woman's work. Yeah, we'd get up as soon as it was daylight, and if we had something special to do we'd get up 'fore daylight. I can remember we just had one old coal oil lamp and we'd try to fix breakfast, and all of us a stumblin' around in the dark.

Q. And you only had one lamp for the entire household?

A. We had two for a while, and one caught far, (fire) down in the bowl, and we throwed it out the window to keep from it catching the house a'far. We'd all be around the fireplace with that one lamp quilting til way in the night. It's a wonder that any of us has got any eyes the way we tried to work.

Q. I suppose you'd work twelve or fifteen hours a day?

A. Oh, yes. We had a center table that we'd set the light on—set it in the middle of the quilt and all of us could get around it, you know, and quilt. We had the old fashion swinging quilting frames that hung from the ceiling. My mother wouldn't quilt on anything else, and I didn't either til you got me over there to that World's Fair.

Q. Now, most of the family was boys, I believe you said.

A. Yeah, they's only three of us girls.

Q. When did you start doing the patchwork quilts—making the patterns?

A. If we got ahold of, or somebody would give us scraps of cloth, why we'd make little squares or nine diamonds or something like that. The first pattern that I really remember her doing, she called it the White Water Beauty. And then somehow she got ahold of the pattern of the Double Wedding Ring. And I've had that pattern ever since I can remember. I've had it over fifty years.

Q. Did you ever come up with patterns of your own?

A. Yeah, we made up a pattern we called it the Nine Diamond. It was nine blocks sewed together. And we would arrange it to have the different colors around, you know—and try to match the colors to make it look pretty.

Q. When did they really start making the quilts with all the different patterns? Do you think they did that a hundred years ago in this part of the country?

A. No, they didn't have all these patterns like that. They had the Grandmother's Flower Garden and the Lone Star, Double Wedding Ring, Bow Tie, and the Nine Diamond. It was after I was married that we went into all these different patterns. 'Course they might've been out there but I just hadn't been nowhere to find them. (Laughs)

Q. Now, the question that I'm always curious about, is when they started tearing up and making them in little pieces and strips—whether they did that because they were just getting scraps here and there, or to make it look prettier?

A. Yeah, we liked to make it look pretty. People would give us scraps, and mother would make our clothing, and we would buy material, and we would save all of that we could get. And we'd make it as pretty as we could, arranged with the colors we had. You didn't have all the pretty materials back then as we do now. All the old clothing that we had, we'd get down and tear it up, you know, and save ever little piece, and then we'd separate it into different piles, you know. And then like if we had enough to make a whole strip for the quilt, then we'd make strips.

It didn't matter too much about the color back then, we was just gonna use them on our beds. But if we wanted to make it for somebody else we'd try and arrange the colors to match.

Q. How long would it take you to quilt a quilt?

A. Me and my two sisters and my mother could quilt one in a day if we really worked at it. And it would take a little longer to piece it—maybe two days.

Q. How much did you get for a quilt back then?

A. We'd quilt a whole quilt for $1.00 and then it raised up to $2.00. We'd get $1.00 for piecing one if they was furnishing the material. People would bring a big bag of quilt pieces and mother would piece all the quilt tops she could get out of it, you know. She saved ever little scrap.

Q. What did you use for the filler?

A. We'd just use two or three plys of old tops we'd sewed together.

Q. Well, would people come there to buy them or would you take them out to sell?

A. They'd come. When people would come and bring work for us to do, why, if we had anything that they liked, they'd buy it.

Q. Did you say once that you and some of the girls, and maybe the boys, would take the quilts around—deliver them to the people?

A. Yes, if they ordered something and we'd get it done, you know, if they lived in walking distance we'd take 'em to them. But mostly what sellin' we done was when the women would come to pick up their quilts that they'd left for us to quilt, then they'd see what we had, and if we had anything they wanted, then they'd buy it.

Q. Mostly you wouldn't have enough scraps yourself and you were quilting for other people that would bring their own scraps in. How come they wouldn't do their own quilting?

A. Well, I guess they's better off than we was. I don't know. And then there's some women that wouldn't dare stick theirselves up with quilting if they could get somebody else to do it.

Q. Where did they come from; around Laurel Grove mostly?

A. Yeah, and Briceville and Oliver Springs, and there were people from across the mountain over in the New River sections.

Q. Did you do the real close intricate stitching?

A. Yeah, we done real good stitching, but we didn't know all these new ways to quilt. I don't think we ever quilted one by the piece, like I quilt now. It was in fans.

Q. Well, if it took four of you three days to piece and quilt a quilt, and if you only got $2.00 for it, my calculation is that each of you got about 17 cents per day — or just slightly over a penny an hour.

A. (She laughs) Yeah, I've worked a many a day in the corn field for O. Z. Duncan for 25 cents a day. Worked for him once seven days in a row for 25 cents a day. We just tried to make enough money to buy sugar and coffee....things that we didn't raise. We growed our own corn to make our own cornmeal, and we'd usually have enough to do. But there was lots of time that we didn't have flour. We didn't have money to buy flour with.

Q. Ate cornbread three meals a day?

A. Well, they's a long time that we didn't have that. We'd have baked potatoes for bread. We didn't have any bread. A lot of time we had baked potatoes when we'd be out of cornmeal. We'd just have baked potatoes and bake them with the skins on.

Q. Did you have to stay out of school to work?

A. Oh, yeah. I wanted to go to school so bad. But in the winter it was cold and snowy and I didn't have no shoes. Sometimes I'd tie rags around my feet when I's just a little girl and wear a pair of mother's old shoes. It'd almost kill me when I couldn't go to school.

Q. You didn't have any shoes of your own?

A. No. Well, I finally got an old ragged second-hand pair of high topped shoes. I guess you remember the old Red Goose shoes. When they's snow on the ground my brothers would go along in front and make tracks for me to walk in. That's how bad I wanted to get an education. I'd cry to get to school. I wound up gettin' a little education, which some of 'em didn't.

I went to the fourth grade. I got *through* the fourth grade, but I had to miss a lot because Mother had to have us a lot. Had to work on the farm there. I guess I got more schoolin' than any of the younger kids did because I'd throw a fit to go.

Q. Wasn't any welfare back then, huh?

A. No, they wasn't nothing back then.

Q. Well, I guess a lot of families were almost starved out.

A. Well, if we hadn't worked and made everthing—we growed s'much—clay peas, beans, and we had some shuck beans. Then we growed beans that we shelled, and had dried beans. They wasn't no way of keepin' things like they are now either. We'd have dried apples, smoked apples, pickled corn, pickled beans. You couldn't hardly can anything and keep it back then.

Q. Were smoked apples the same as sulphured apples?

A. Yeah. We just called them smoked apples. And big barrels of kraut. And whatever we could can you know, like berries. A lot of times we'd sweeten berries and things with molasses. We'd make molasses every year. Raise the cane. We had a rule in the summertime to put up one mess of something every day. If we had to go out and get a few apples and cook them and can 'em; well whatever. We'd put up a mess of something every day. Mother would call it a "mess" of something.

Q. Apples or beans or kraut?

A. Yeah, something every day. And o'course we held our cabbage up back then. Make a big hole in the ground for cabbage, potatoes, and turnips. Mother would take the small cabbage plants up that had small heads, pull 'em up roots and all. Then she'd throw them in this big hole we'd dig and put straw around it. Then when we'd get it full, we'd put straw back over the top of it and cover it up with dirt, then put planks over it. Put the planks so that it wouldn't leak down in there, and we'd go out during the winter and just get pretty white cabbage heads. They's the best you ever eat.

Q. Your mother must have been a good manager.

A. Yes, she was—she had to be. If she hadn't have had the know-how, we'd a never survived, 'cause she knowed what to tell us to do and what not to do.

Q. Back to the quilting, did you ever do any applique type quilting?

A. Oh yes.

Q. When did you start doing that?

A. That was after I was married. I never saw anything appliqued til I was around 25 or something like that. The way we applique today is to take a sewing machine and zig-zag it on. But, we did it by hand back then.

Q. And you never started doing that until after you were grown?

A. No, I don't remember ever seeing any of it til I was grown, the applique work.

Q. Well, there's another process where they go in from the back, between where they sew, between where they stitch, and push cotton in there.

A. They call that tuffin' (tufting). Yeah, where you'd push cotton in there, we'd call it tuffin'.

Q. How would you get it in there?

A. Well, I didn't do any of it til I was grown. I put a little piece of cotton down on the quilt top and put that little piece of material down on the cotton and just tack it down with my fingers, and then I'd take and embroider around it. Course that's pretty hard to do, but it's pretty when you get it done. Then after you quilt it, the flowers that you put that cotton in would stand a way up, you know, like you could pick them off. I've done that - that's what we call tuffin'.

Q. When did you start making quilts on your own? After you got married?

A. Un-huh, yeah. After I got married I've quilted a quilt out in a day for myself. My husband was working for Tennessee Valley Authority and he'd leave 'fore daylight and get in after dark, and I'd put a quilt out sometimes 'fore daylight and that night I'd have that quilt done. I was s'glad to have something to work with that I just went to making quilts right away. Everbody around there was so surprised at me!

Q. How many quilts have you made per year on the average, would you say?

A. I really don't know. I've sold this year—I've sold two thousand and ten dollars, and eight cents worth this year.

Q. In one year?

A. Un-huh. I never kept account of 'em. My granddaughter got me a calendar to keep account of everything I do this year. I said, 'Wait til I get 69 year old, and then start keepin' a record!'

Q. I guess you've made more in the last few years than you've ever made?

A. Yes. After I began sellin' them. O'course now I've sold quilts for years, but after I found out that I could sell a lot more, I've been making a lot more.

Me and some other women went down there to Fratersville Baptist Church, back in the 30's, I think it was, and we made enough money quilting to pay for concreting the whole floor of the basement, putting in a new ceiling, and gettin' benches made for the church.

We'd start work of a morning and we'd work all day, and sometimes we'd go home and eat supper then come back and quilt of a night.

People would bring us the material and we'd do the quilting for $5.00 a quilt, and give the money to the church. We did this for several months—until we had enough money to pay for fixin' up the church.

Then when we got ready to start spending it, some of the men wanted to tell us how to do it. Thought we didn't have enough sense to decide how to spend it. I told them that the women had enough sense to set there and freeze theirselves half to death and make the money, and that they had enough sense to decide how to spend it.

Q. Do you remember the first quilt that you sold that you made yourself?

A. Yes. It was appliqued tulip.

Q. That was after you married?

A. I sold a hundred chances at 50 cents a chance and got $50.00 out of it. The first one I ever sold.

Q. That was pretty good back then, wasn't it?

A. Yeah it was real good! 'Course they was a lot of work to it. It was all appliqued by hand—the tulip. That was the first one I ever sold.

Q. Do you have any quilts that you and your mother and your sisters made?

A. Yeah, I have one that my mother pieced, but I didn't quilt it til long after she died. I've got it on my bed now.

Q. They didn't have the pretty quilts in your area, you have said?

A. No, they wasn't pretty quilts to go on top (of the bed) because they didn't have the patterns and things to do with back then.

Q. Do you always use a thimble?

A. Well, now a lot of people quilt without it, but I never could. I started using a thimble—Lord, I guess I started when I started sewing. You really have to learn how to use them.

Q. Did all the old people use thimbles? Do you remember?

A. Yeah, but they didn't use the type they use now. The first ones that I remember didn't have any end in them. You had to push it (the needle) through with the side of your finger. I push my needle on the end of mine, is the way I use mine now.

Q. Did you ever wear a needle out?

A. I certainly have. I used one needle three years, that my mother-in-law gave me when my husband and I got married. It was a little sharp, blunted needle that had a real good eye in it, and I quilted and used that needle for three years. Kept up with it. And now I lose them. You can't buy good quiltin' needles like you use to, either.

Q. Well, what happened to that one. Did you wear the back off of it where you put the....

A. No, wore the point til the point would bend. You know you couldn't stick it through.

Q. Did you ever sharpen the point?

A. Yes, I have.

Q. How do you sharpen it?

A. Well, I take a file or a whet rock and rub on it. We have had needles to rust and we'd put them down on the floor and roll them with our feet on the floor to get the rust off of them.

Q. Your mother didn't have any trouble getting you all to work did she?

A. No, she never did have any. They wasn't any of us lazy. I was never lazy, that's one thing I can say. I stay at something if it—I do something even if it is wrong sometimes. (She laughs)

Q. Well, I think people that keep busy enjoy themselves a lot more than the ones that just sit around.

A. If I hadn't had some talent—and I didn't have enough education to have a great talent—if I hadn't a knew how to sew and make quilts and things like that, I couldn't have survived after my husband died. Because I missed him so much and it stayed on my mind so much that I......and when I had something to keep me busy, I didn't have so much time to think about it.

OPAL HATMAKER'S WORLD'S FAIR QUILT

During the 1982 World's Fair in Knoxville, I had occasion to recommend and even sponsor some traditional mountain folk to appear at the Stokely Folklife Festival there. Opal Hatmaker was one of those I recommended. She spent an entire week there quilting while people from around the world observed and talked with her.

After the last day of the fair was over and I was driving her home, I asked if she had enjoyed it. Her response was spontaneous, believable, and moving. "That was the most enjoyable week that I ever spent in my life. I never enjoyed a week so much — nor met so many nice people."

Opal wanted to do something to show her appreciation. It was for this reason she made this quilt — the World's Fair quilt, for my wife and me. It is interesting and significant, I think, but not surprising, that Opal, who has quilted since she was 8 years old, would select a quilt as the ultimate manner in expressing appreciation.

LUCY STOOKSBURY
"Laziness has killed more people than hard work"

One of the most common family names in the northeast part of Anderson County, Tennessee, and in the adjoining counties of Campbell and Union, is Stooksbury. They trace their ancestry back to one Lord Stooksbury, an Englishman whose son William came to America in early colonial times. William's grandson Robin came into this frontier area from Virginia shortly after 1800, and is presumably the progenitor of all the Stooksburys in this immediate area. Tradition has it these Stooksbury's intermarried with the Cherokee Indians.

A few miles north of the village of Andersonville, in an area known as the Ridges, lives Lucy Stooksbury in the ancestral homeplace. Lucy has outlived all the old folks, and now lives alone on the remote homestead. Although she is now frail, and in ill health, she remains fiesty, witty, and an incessant talker. I told her of my interest in quilts, and thus sparked an immediate and enthusiastic harangue.

The first quilt I ever quilted was Around the World. Lena Robbins lived down the road here, and she come and stayed with us twenty somethin' years. I give her the pieces and she pieced this Round the World quilt—she just wanted somethin' to do. And when she got it pieced I quilted it. And they's a woman come in here a few years ago and wanted to buy it. And I sold it to her and then I hauled off and pieced me another one and quilted it.

Uncle Joe stayed here with me and Daddy for forty-five years, and Daddy died and left him here with me. And I took care of him after that for nineteen years—til he died. He had two strokes, and I'd have to stay close by, and I'd quilt. I used to piece quilts til 12 o'clock. I'd do my sleepin' of a morning. I still yet sleep of a morning.

Lord, I couldn't tell you how many quilts I have made. I've give Johnny's children all one. I made an old Wild Rose and took it to the fair in Clinton and won second place. That's the prettiest thing you ever saw.

We used to have an old iron kettle out here we washed in, you know. That's the way we done all our washin', and then I got rich in '39 and got this here 'lectricity in here. Bought me a washing machine, a Speed Queen and used it thirty-five years and the bottom come out. And I went down here at Daugherty's and got me another Speed Queen. Paid $99.00 for the old one and the new one cost $139.00. Shows you what a change they is. And these shoes I've got on cost $26.00. You used to get a pair like this for two or three dollars.

They's not many women around here makes quilts anymore—run up and down the road in these here automobiles and don't have no time fer nothin'. Laziness has killed more people than hard work. But they've gone back to it (making quilts) down here in Oak Ridge. They say they're makin' quilts like everything.

LUCY STOOKSBURY'S WALL HANGING QUILT SQUARE

"My aunt over here in Knox County, her name was Dunis Hill McHafey, I'd go over there and stay a week or two at a time with her. She didn't have no children. One day, it was 1927, she wanted me and her to make something, and we made that there quilt square and I had it framed and I've kept it ever since."

LUCY STOOKSBURY'S
WOOL LINED QUILT

"I used to help Daddy raise sheep. One time they was one of our sheep that got tangled up in the wire fence up here next to the Louie Nelson place and it couldn't get out and it died. I found it up there dead and I pulled the wool from it by the handful. I took that wool and washed it, cleaned it, and carded it, and used it for batten for this quilt, The Irish Chain, and I've used that quilt all these years. That was back in the twenties when I made it."

BERNICE HENSLEY OF INDIAN FORK
(Unicoi County, Tennessee)

If you're heading for Asheville, North Carolina from Erwin, Tennessee, going up Indian Fork, you may notice a crudely lettered sign which reads "Calico Quilts."If this doesn't get your attention, the arrow above it pointing upward at a 45° angle should. There's a reason for the arrow's odd angle; it is designed to draw attention to the white farm house on a sizeable hill a few hundred yards off the road at the foot of a laurel-covered mountain.

It was almost dark when we arrived, and I wasn't sure anyone was home. But when I got to the front porch I smelled country ham frying. It wasn't long before Bernice Hensley came to the door, a hand-made towel in her hand and a smile on her face.

I told her what we were doing. She turned her supper off and invited us to a small upstairs room where her suspended quilting frame filled the entire space. She started quilting for us, and never slowed as I queried her. I asked her about the quilt she was working on, how long she had been a quilter, and what she charged for quilting.

Oh, I've worked on this one ever since last summer, and I've still got a couple of months to go. I'll get, if I'm lucky, 25 cents an hour, and them's hard hours. Time I buy the material, and law! it's expensive. I'll do well to get that much. This here one is supposed to go to a woman in New Jersey. Says she's going to take it. I've got her name and address and I'm supposed to let her know when it's finished.

I've got me a T.V. set in here and when you see some long, ugly stitching (in the quilt), why then you know they's something that come on that I wanted to watch (laughter). I wear this here shade to protect my eyes. After a few hours, my eyes gets sort of tired.

I asked her if she liked to quilt, and this brought a quick, positive reply - and a smile to her face.

Oh, boy! I love to quilt. I garden and work in the yard a lot when it's warm and in the summer, but in the winter I quilt. I enjoy quilting more than anythang I ever done.

I learnt to quilt from my mother, and she's still quilting. Past 90 and still quilting. I was raised up here on the Holston River at Emmet, near Bristol. I was a Hensley 'fore I married—and I married a Hensley. Yeah, I like to quilt. Get up here in this attic room and just set and quilt all by myself. Nobody to bother me. I'd druther quilt than anything I ever done.

"I've worked on this one since last summer and I've still got two months to go. I'll get, if I'm lucky, 25 cents an hour." Bernice Hensley had this Double Wedding Ring quilt up the day we visited her.

Bernice admires the Log Cabin quilt she had recently finished. Hanging in the window behind her are a number of ribbons she has won on her quilts in various shows.

Chapter VI

Old Homesteads and Their Quilts

When a person admires the beauty, art, and workmanship of a quilt he surely wonders about its background, the people who made it, and the location and type of home from which it came. Yet, it is often impossible to learn anything about the history of old quilts.

While one cannot ascertain information about quilts which have passed through several hands, it is possible to learn something of the background of similar type quilts through documenting where the type is most often found today. For example, a two-story antebellum home located on a prosperous farm in a wide fertile valley may tend to contain a certain type and quality quilt, while a log cabin on a steep ridge with small acreage and poor land may tend to produce an entirely different type.

After visiting many old homesteads, one can almost predict the type, quality, and number of quilts that will be found there. However, there are always surprises, and this uncertainty adds to the anticipation of exploring such places.

The locations of the old homes, the economic status of the families through the years, and conversations with relatives of the quilters, all add to the background of the quilts. A glimpse at the following family homesteads will provide some insight into the people, places, and circumstances connected with the quilts and may shed information about similar quilts with unknown backgrounds.

Inside this peaceful log homestead were stored scores of quilts, made here by the Bakers and their kin, some soon after the house was built in the 1830's. When Robin Hood and I arrived here in January 1983, we found 80 year old Henry going in for dinner with his ax and a load of firewood.

THE BAKER QUILTS

As I drove down Thomas Weaver Road in rural Knox County, Tennessee, I was impressed with the large number of new homes that had been built, and the old homes that had been torn away since the time I walked there as a barefoot boy. But I knew that the old Baker place would be the same. I couldn't imagine it would ever change.

Sure enough, when it came into view this stately homeplace seemed precisely the same as when I first saw it almost half a century ago — the same, I am informed, as when my mother was a girl and when my grandfather was a child. Indeed it is little changed from the time when the Bakers built it in the frontier wilderness several generations ago. The bee hives sat on a bluff above the creek just as when my brother and I, as toddlers, mistook the bees for house flies and attempted to kill them with wooden paddles. I still remember the baking soda Aunt Jane applied to the stings, as well as the tobacco cuds the men reluctantly relinquished for the same purpose.

Virtually all Homo sapiens emulate their neighbors, doing that which is fashionable at the time rather than that which is reasonable. Because of this characteristic, most of the old ways and the old relics are abandoned along the way as one faddish thing after another appears on the scene—to be re-discovered and eagerly sought after by later generations. Corner cupboards, pie safes, and harvest tables, relegated to the smokehouse, wood shed or other out-buildings, are examples. Discarded as worthless relics by our grandparents, they are cherished as beautiful and utilitarian treasures by many of the present generation.

The Baker family members are not average folk. Most of the reasonably prosperous pioneer families expected the stop-gap log house to be replaced within a few years, or certainly by the second generation, by a frame or a brick home. But the Baker family simply added onto their log cabin — and have lived there til the present day. Much of the furniture and many of the farm and household items of a hundred and fifty years ago are either still being used or remain in the spot where they were last used. Fifty years ago, their neighbors may have ridiculed their quaint customs, their old, unpainted log house, their molasses making, and their lack of progress. Now they are the envy of the younger generation, many of whom are either reconstructing old log homes or are purchasing new ones from one of the many companies "manufacturing" log houses.

Tiny Baker, at 92, looks pensive as she admires the beauty in the quilt her grandmother made almost one hundred fifty years ago. "Her name was Susan Branson Baker, and I've always understood that she made this quilt soon after her and Grandpap got married in the 1830's — right here in this old log house." It is appliqued and pieced, and is expertly and minutely quilted.

The quilt shown lying on top of the cabinet was made by Eula's great-aunt, Ella Hill. The one to the right was made by his grandmother Baker, and the Double Wedding Ring pieced quilt was made by his mother Jane Rice Baker. Aunt Jane, my grandfather's sister, is shown, along with her husband preacher Tom Baker, in the photograph hanging on the wall directly over the quilts.

Now, in 1983, the plowed garden, the woodpile, the great log house, and the little stream that runs a few feet away from the pioneer home have, it seems, defied time. As I walked across the wide porch I could see Tiny Baker sitting by the wide, wood-burning fireplace. Tiny, the daughter of Uncle Tom and Aunt Jane Rice Baker, has lived her 91 years in the old home, as did her ancestors. She lives with her brother Henry, and his wife Eula.

Eula invited me in. I was surprised that Tiny recognized me so quickly, almost, I thought, before she could see me. "Well, that's Rice. We've been a wondering whatever happened to you," she said.

After inquiring about the health of our respective families, I raised the subject of quilts. "They's a few old quilts around here somewhere," Eula laughed. "I'll see if I can find some of them." She darted upstairs to fetch them.

I followed Eula up the sturdy steps and into a large room where she laid the lid off the largest quilt chest I've ever seen. It was fully eight feet long, almost three feet wide, and as deep. It was completely filled with fine old quilts neatly packed in their safe storage place.

I later learned there was another chest, almost as large, also filled with quilts. There were at least twenty patchwork and applique quilts, most of which had striking colors, beautiful patterns, and minute stitching, and deemed to be over 100 years old, and some much older.

When we started examining them, having taken them downstairs before the open fireplace, each one we unfolded seemed more beautiful than the last. Every one reminded Tiny and Eula of Aunt Jane, or Granny Hill, or Grandma Baker. I remarked about the excellent condition of the quilts, and asked about their use. Both Tiny and Eula laughed, and said they had never been used.

"They've laid away up there packed in the old quilt boxes, some them for nearly a hundred years, I guess," said Tiny. "Oh, they may have used them a few times as bedspreads when special company came, or when somebody died—but mostly they've just been packed away as keepsakes."

I asked Tiny what happened to all the quilts made by her mother, and by her grandmothers. She mentioned those given to various members of the family, and some that were presented to destitute neighbors. I asked if they ever sold any.

"Oh, no, they never sold quilts," she said as if it would have been a sinful act. "No, they give a lot away—but I never heard of them ever selling a quilt."

Susan Branson Baker, shown here with her husband Anderson, made some of the oldest quilts at the Baker homeplace. They are the grandparents of Henry and Tiny. Her quilting would have been done primarily in the mid-1800's.

Aunt Jane Rice Baker is shown here with her husband Tom and their children in an old photograph taken in the early part of this century. The children, from the left are: Henry, Lloyd (being held by his father) Tiny, and Becky. Henry and Tiny are the only two survivors of the family. (Photograph courtesy Henry and Tiny Baker)

LONE STAR AND DOUBLE
WEDDING RING

The Lone Star was among dozens of beautiful and expertly made old quilts stored in the large quilt chests in an unfinished upstairs room. It is interesting to note the incorporation of the Double Wedding Ring pattern surrounding the star. As pointed out earlier, I was informed by Chris Keys of White County, Tennessee, that it was bad luck for someone to receive a Lone Star quilt as a gift if there was not some other pattern included. Henry and his wife Eula are shown holding it outside the Baker house.

One would be hard pressed to decide which is the most impressive feature of this quilt, the appliqued pattern, or the quilted designs. It was brought down from its upstairs storage box in the old log house, and placed upon the hand-turned bed to be photographed.

THE DUTCH VALLEY QUILTS

Dutch Valley is one of the most interesting and picturesque little valleys in East Tennessee. It stretches roughly from the town of Oliver Springs north-easterly to Lake City, once called Coal Creek. Towering over this fertile valley is Cumberland Mountain (locally called Walnut Ridge) almost as wild and untamed as when the first settlers came into the region one hundred seventy-five years ago.

The Valley takes it's name for the *Deutsch* (German) who settled there about 1799 or 1800. This group of German settlers were led by one Frederick Sadler, a wagonmaker from York, Pennsylvania. Sadler came there with his seven German sons-in-law and their families: Shanliver, Bumgartner, Claxton, Clodfelter, Leinart, Lieb, and Spessard.

The three homes we visited in Dutch Valley all produced quilts of a superior quality. These were the type of quilts which one would except to find in the relatively well-to-do home located on large farms. They are not the type usually found in small mountain cabins. However, this postulation does not always hold true. Log cabins may contain beautiful quilts, as has been observed earlier, although they tend to be patchwork rather than applique. A brief visit to these three homes in a late afternoon in March provided some insight into the type quilts this one mountain valley produced, and gave some indication as to how the present owners cherish these heirlooms.

Helen and Hall Burress, in front of their home which was built by Helen's grandfather, hold one of the family quilts, the Mexican Rose.

THE HALL AND HELEN BURRESS PLACE
(Dutch Valley)

In 1861, Henry P. Farmer sat on a pair of draw bars at what is now called the Burress place, and watched a contingent of Confederate soldiers pass through the valley. One of the troops recognized young Farmer, and said to him; "We'll be marching back from Clinton tomorrow and we'll be expecting you to go with us."

Henry knew that this was no idle invitation, and that he would have no choice but to join the troops when they returned. But his sympathy lay with the Union, and he took to the mountains and persuaded other young men to join him. They walked to the famous Cumberland Gap where they joined the Union Army. Henry enlisted as a private and was mustered out at the end of the war as a lieutenant. He came home to Dutch Valley and soon afterward built the two-story frame house shown here.

Helen Burress, who, with her husband Hall, lives in the house today, is a granddaughter of Henry Farmer. She is also a descendant of the Dunkins whose ancestral home was also in Dutch Valley.

The numerous quilts which Helen owns were made by these two old Dutch Valley families; the Farmers and the Dunkins. Although Helen cherishes them very much, she doesn't know which quilts belonged to which family.

The spring sun is good for quilts as well as the beagle. These three are among the several ancestral quilts Helen Burress laid out for us to view.

THE OLD FOWLER PLACE

Perhaps the most historic house in Dutch Valley is the old Fowler home. It was built in the early 1800's by the Edwards family out of brick made only a hundred yards from the house site. Samuel Fowler bought the place in 1901, and it came to be known as the Fowler place. It is listed in the National Register of Historic Places as the Edwards-Fowler home.

When I told Sam (son of Samuel) and his wife Bertha of my interest in old quilts, Bertha chose a Feathered Star to show us. There were many more packed in the upstairs chests, but she thought this one the most interesting and historic.

It was made by Sam's grandmother Emily Caroline Trotter Robertson, and her sister Jane Trotter Walker. They were originally from Sevier County, Tennessee. Emily gave the quilt to her daughter Mary Lee Robertson Fowler, and upon her death, it fell to Sam. Bertha recalls that her mother-in-law would often unpack the quilt and show it, but that she never used it.

Sam and Bertha Fowler hold the Feathered Star quilt made by Sam's grandmother and stored in the old Fowler house shown in the background.

Emily Caroline Trotter Robertson, who made the Feathered Star quilt in the late 1800's. (Photograph courtesy of Sam and Bertha Fowler)

MAXINE AND EDMOND SHANLEVER
(with quilts made
by their grandmothers)

Maxie Shanlever, 86 years young, and her brother Edmond Shanlever are shown here at their Dutch Valley, Tennessee home with two quilts made by their grandmothers. The one on the left was made by their grandmother Coward. The Cowards lived between Clinton and Oak Ridge on the Clinch River and were an early and prominent family of Anderson County. The Coward farm lay on both sides of the river necessitating the use of a ferry to get to and from the portion of land on the opposite side.

Maxie stated that her grandfather Coward died when he was only 42, and that her grandmother had nine children to raise. She wasn't sure how old the quilt was, but was positive that it was "well over a hundred years old."

The quilt folded at the right was made by Talitha Moore Shanlever, the paternal grand-mother of Maxie and Edmond. She also lived on the Clinch River. The Moores, too, were an old and prominent family of the area, becoming large coal mining operators in later years.

"I don't know how old this quilt is," Maxie said, "but it's been here a lot longer than I have."

"How long has that been?" I asked, in an endeavor to learn her age. She was too smart for such elemental subtlety. "A long time," she replied. She did eventually divulge that she had been living in the valley for eighty-six years. For forty-two of those years she was a school teacher — known by thousands of students as Miss Maxie.

Both quilts are believed to date from the 1850-1870 period. "They were used very little," Maxie recalls. "I remember my mother hanging them out to air in the spring of the year. I thought they were pretty, but after Mother died they were pretty much left packed away for all these years. But here of late I appreciate them more. I get them out and look at them more than I used to."

PENNSYLVANIA SWATCH QUILT

Agnes Gounder and her husband operated a hotel in Orwingsburg, Pennsylvania, in the late 1800's which was frequented by traveling salesmen, or drummers as they were commonly called. Many of these drummers sold suits and other clothing, and they carried with them small strips of the cloth as samples of the material from which the garments were made. These were called swatches, and Agnes Gounder, being the frugal German she was, collected these swatches from her guests and made them into a quilt.

On this quilt, the infinite variety of flowers, horeseshoes, etc., are embroidered with crewel type stitching. The center square is six times as large as the other squares and contains the date 1895, a number of flowers, and the very ornate and highly embellished letters "R.K.M." which were the initials of Agnes's mother, Rebecca K. Meyer, for whom the quilt was made. When her mother died, the quilt came back to Agnes, and

upon her death the quilt went to her daughter Mae Agnes Gounder Lovett. She later gave it to her son, James E. Lovett, who lived in Georgia and South Carolina before joining the Tennessee Valley Authority in Knoxville as an engineer. James later worked as an engineer with other firms, and founded two business of his own. He is currently director of the Air Pollution Control Department, Knox County, Tennessee.

James remembers hearing stories that indicated his grandmother Agnes was pretty much the manager of the family. He recalls having heard, on more than one occasion, that Grandpa Gounder went off to Philadelphia, became involved with race horses and such, and traded the hotel for what he thought was a fine racehorse, which proved to be a worthless nag. Grandma Gounder was not at all happy about that.

Chapter VII

Quilts With Stories to Tell

It is hard to imagine any type of household item which, collectively or individually, convey such interesting, warm, and personal stories as do quilts. Virtually every quilt has a background composed of the human involvement, the love, and the labor which went into its creation. Unfortunately, the intimate details of the life of a quilt are seldom known, but occasionally fragmented stories regarding the quilts have been passed down from earlier generations. Some of these stories are most interesting and revealing.

Attempts have been made to authenticate the accuracy of the histories and folk stories connected with certain quilts. While some of the stories have been passed along with the quilt itself from one generation to another, the stories probably have been changed somewhat over the years. One may assume, however, that the stories had a basis in fact, and knowing that the stories were considered worthy of telling so many times is itself significant.

THE FLAG QUILT
(Circled Star)

Although the woman who made this quilt lived in Tullahoma, in the southern part of Middle Tennessee near the Alabama line, both her husband and son fought with the Union side during the Civil War. She wanted to make a patriotic quilt based on the United States flag, but she did not want to incur the wrath of Southern sympathizers by having it resemble a Yankee flag in color and design.

So, she made a red, white and blue quilt, which contained the stars and stripes, but changed the configuration so that one would not readily discern it was based on the U.S. flag. This is a concept similar to that employed by Amanda McDowell in making her "concealed" flag.

This is believed to be an original design and to have been made about 1860. The backing is made of homespun fabric, and it has borders only on two sides. It was made for a bed that was to be positioned against a wall.

Allison Arnold bought the quilt from the great-granddaughter of its maker, and presented it to her husband as an anniversary present. It has since appeared in the magazine, *Lady's Circle Patchwork Quilts,* and has hung in the McClung Museum in Knoxville during the 1982 World's Fair. (Photographed at the Museum of Appalachia)

THE FLAG
THAT WAS HIDDEN IN A QUILT

Curtis McDowell was principal of a small subscriptive school called Cumberland Institute in the Middle Tennessee mountains near the town of Sparta during the Civil War. Although he had sons in both the Northern and Southern Armies, McDowell retained allegiance to the United States Government, and he faced a formidable decision. He could continue to fly the United States flag (or hide it for later use) and almost surely have his school and perhaps his family destroyed by the Confederates; or he could destroy the flag, assume a neutral position, and be relatively safe from the ravages of both sides. He chose, instead, another alternative, more palatable, imaginative, and certainly more romantic.

He and his daughter Amanda chose to retain the flag, but to conceal it in such a manner as to insure that it could never be found. Amanda cut the flag into thousands of half-inch square pieces and made it into a Triple Irish Chain quilt that bore no resemblance to the design of the flag. The flag, in this transformed state, could be openly displayed even in front of Confederate soldiers. None ever suspected this quilt was in fact Old Glory.

The quilt remains in the possession of the McDowell family, belonging to Jack McDowell, a chemist who lives near Oak Ridge in Anderson County, Tennessee. Equally as interesting is the fact that the details of this event were recorded by Amanda McDowell herself in the form of a diary which she kept throughout this period. This diary is also in the possession of Jack and Betty McDowell.

The diary is in good condition except for numerous lines which have been carefully cut from the pages. The story is that Amanda had referred to Larkin Craig, her lover, in these lines. After the two parted company, and Amanda married another man, she went back and removed all the amorous allusions to him.

This diary was used as a basis for a historical novel called *Fiddles In The Cumberlands,* written and published by Lela McDowell Blankenship, Amanda's niece. The following account is from this book and is accompanied by a footnote from the author.

At the school there had so far been quiet, but it was well known that a division of sentiment smoldered among the students. Perhaps Curtis McDowell had been given more consideration because it was apparent that his two sons were divided on their opinion of the national crisis, Fayette siding warmly with the Confederates and Jack taking a decided stand against secession. But in spite of this escape from the maurauding element that had kept the valley in an uproar, Amanda and Mary always dreaded a visit from sympathizers of either side. One evening they heard hoofs clatter to a stop at the gate in front of their home and gave each other a look of dread before they went together to the door. Their father was meeting with some students at the schoolhouse and they expected to direct the riders there. They were surprised to see the schoolhouse showing no sign of life and the men dismounting to come in.

"Is McDowell here?" one of the Confederate soldiers inquired, and the girls saw that he had the flag from the school house — the flag Amanda had so carefully made when the debating societies had requested it.

"He is not here," Amanda said calmly, but her hand went out toward the latch of the door.

"Well, we can leave this, and our message here!" As the leader said that, he tore the flag across and dropped it to the ground and the two or three of them stamped it with their boots. "Tell McDowell that is the way we feel about his flag, and he had better keep it down."

They had learned early in the distrubance to have as little to say as possible, so they made no answer but stepping backward enough to close the door and slide the heavy latch into place. They heard the men remount and all turn toward the valley with a great clatter and shouting.

A few minutes later their father and some students came up. The girls felt a great relief. They had feared their father would not take the insult quietly. But he too had known what was best and he had kept back in one of the cabins where he had gone instead of the schoolhouse as they had believed.

Sorrowfully Amanda gathered up the torn flag and took it into the house. She stored it in the chest after cleaning the mud footprints away and said that later she and Mary would make it into a quilt.

This is an actual happening that has been told in the presence of our family many times. I now have the quilt made from the blue and white of the flag pieced by Amanda - and Mrs. Monroe Bartlett had the red and white quilt pieced by Mary. — Lela McDowell Blankenship.

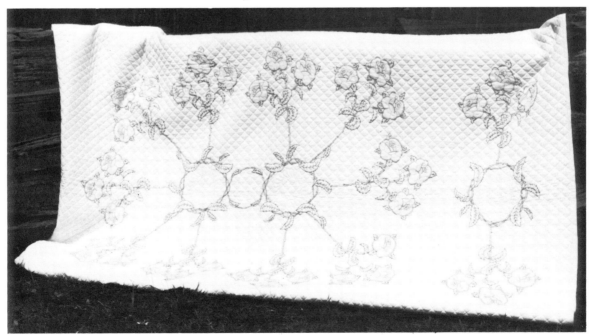

THE TABLE CLOTH QUILT

"My mother had a table cloth with a pretty rose on it, and she got the idea of making a quilt using that pattern," Chris Keys pointed out.

"She just drew this pattern, the Satin Stitch Rose, she called it. Then she embroidered it, and then quilted it."

THE "ONE-HAND" QUILT
(Crany, West Virginia)

Crany, West Virginia, was located in Wyoming County, on the Clear Fork of the Guyandot River. It was a most remote area, and like many late and inaccessible frontier areas, it is now void of people and has returned to its original state of nature. One of the few reminders of the several generations of people who lived there is this quilt. It is most remarkable in that it was quilted by a woman who was almost totally crippled in her right hand. It was displayed in the 1983 Museum of Appalachia Quilt Show by Knoxville business-man Ed Lambert, its present owner, and grandson of the lady who made it. Ed himself tells of its history:

Dan Gunnoe and his bride, Etta Marshall, built their home in Crany just above the "Marshall Place" on Clear Fork of the Guyandot River. As the years faded away, the Gunnoes raised four boys and three girls and "Uncle Dan," as the community affectionately called him, became the postmaster and the most affluent man in the area. One by one the children left their hearthside until only memories warmed there. Today the home is gone and nothing remains except on a nearby knoll grown thick with greenbriar and other bramble there are markers on the graves of some 30 or 40 of the pioneers of the area. Dan and Etta's graves are the most prominent in the cemetery being situated under an old cedar tree whose thick foliage has prevented any under-growth on their resting places.

Before Etta passed on in 1929, she made a quilt for each of her surviving children. This quilt was made for her daughter Lake. Her right hand was paralyzed in a closed position and she inserted the needle by holding it with the knuckles of her ring and middle finger. Her left hand did most of the work. The quilt belonged to Lake, the mother of its present owner, who died at age 86 in 1965. She used the quilt in her home for more than 40 years.

Lake's quilt is 70" x 72". The design is a variation of a common pattern of the day, "Pine Tree." There are six or seven stitches to the inch and the rows of stitches are a half-inch apart. The quilting alone has an estimated 60,000 stitches not including the patch work.

Crany is gone. The old house and furnishings are gone. Dan and Etta are gone. Their children are gone -- but the love that Etta put in these quilts and the warmth they emit are still with us.

Dan and Etta Gunnoe are shown in a photograph reproduced from one taken in 1928. Etta made this fine quilt for her daughter using only her left hand, as her right one was paralyzed in a closed position. (Courtesy of their grandson, Ed Lambert.)

THE SALT BAG QUILT
(Coiled Rattlesnake)

In going through the packed-away quilts in the John Carrico home, daughter Star Carrico commented on each one as she removed it from the chest or from the dresser drawer. "Now, this one was made by Daddy's Aunt Lareu Lawson. She made it out of salt bags. Back then they sold salt in cloth bags and she saved them up and finally got enough to make herself a quilt. She called this the "Quiled (coiled) Rattlesnake" quilt."

The pattern is perhaps more generally known as Baby Bunting. This same pattern was found on a quilt at the Ellis Stewart place, and they also called it Quiled Rattlesnake. The Stewart's home on Newman's Ridge in Hancock County is about eighty-five miles form the Carrico home in Scott County, Virginia.

LORA CARRICO AND HER TRAGEDY QUILT

Lora Carrico holds the quilt which her mother pieced for Lora's son Hershly. Lora sadly recalls the story:

"Mother, her name was Avone, but everybody called her Vone, Vone Smith Flanary. She pieced this quilt for our only boy who was killed in a motorcycle wreck in 1947. And after he was killed she just put it up and never finished it. Its laid in there packed away in the back room ever since."

Lora Carrico lives in Scott County, Virginia, about half-way between Gate City and historic Fort Blackmore on the Clinch River. She and her late husband John Carrico, grew up there with the reknowned Mother Maybelle Carter and her family. John was a sawmiller, farmer, carpenter, musician, cornmiller, maker of Kentucky rifles, etc. He was a collector of Indian relics and frontier related items, and had an impressive collection of these artifacts. I learned that Lora has made quilts for most of her life, but had been unable to do so recently because of her health. She lives on the old homeplace with Star, her only living child.

MARTHA STOOKSBURY MEMORIAL QUILT

In the course of the conversation with Bonnie Carden she told me of an old quilt which she thought might be of interest to me; and indeed it was.

Mother had a sister named Martha who died at the age of 19 of typhoid fever, about 1885. Well, she had a nice dress made out of what they called madris cotton, but it was customary to bury people in new clothing; so they made, or had made, a new dress to bury her in. But her mother, that was my grandmother, took that cotton dress, and made it into this quilt.

My grandmother, Sarah Oaks Stooksbury made the quilt from her daughter Martha's dress after she died. She had eight children, and Martha was one of the eight. When my grandmother died in 1914, she gave the quilt to my mother, who kept it all these years, and then she left it for me. You can see that it's been used a lot somewhere along the line, but I don't think Mother ever used it after she got it.

THE LOUISA SHARP STOOKSBURY
MEMORIAL QUILT

I had never heard of the custom of making a quilt from the dress of a recently deceased family member until Bonnie Carden told me of the quilt made from her aunt's dress. On the same day (January 14, 1983) that Bonnie informed me of this incident, my Aunt Willie told me a similar story relating to her grandmother, Louisa Sharp Stooksbury. (Her husband, Lewis Stooksbury, who lived near Loyston in Union County, Tennessee, was a cousin to Martha Stooksbury, for whom the other memorial quilt was made.) Willie told the story as she had heard it so often from her father Lawrence Stooksbury.

Grandmother Stooksbury died during the birth of her fourteenth child. That was in 1897 and she was just 43 years old. She had this dress that was made out of pure silk, or so they said, and Grandmother's daughter, Aunt Pearl, took that dress and made it into this quilt. I guess it was one of those full-length dresses, and it made the entire top of the quilt.

Aunt Pearl was just 15 when her mother died and I think she made the quilt soon afterwards — in 1897 or '98, I guess. She was sickly and never married, and didn't live too long herself. Just before she died she give this quilt to Dad because, she said, she knowed he would take care of it.

Well, he did take good care of it. He never let it be used, and he wouldn't let us kids bother it. And after he died I brought it up here, but I'd like for you to take it and put in your Museum so it can be seen.

I don't know whether or not this practice was widespread, or if it was only a local custom, but it seems a most practical, and respectful, thing to do. The quilt serves as a remembrance of the departed one, and at the same time it serves a useful purpose. It is interesting to note that in both instances, the material was not cut into small pieces, but rather was used in as large sections as possible.

Louisa Sharp Stooksbury.

When Louisa Stooksbury died at the age of 42 with the birth of her fourteenth child, one of her daughters took her silk dress and made it into this quilt upon which her great-great-granddaughter Missy Irwin is shown. The bed also belonged to Lewis and Louisa Stooksbury.

ALBUM BLOCK STATE QUILT

I acquired this quilt many years before I had any appreciable interest in the subject, and before I maintained copious notes as to the origin and background on the items I bought. My information on this quilt is based on memory. It was purchased from Guy Bowers of Kingsport, Tennessee, who stated that the woman who made it was the daughter of a man from that area who had, in the era of the Wright brothers, invented an airplane. Guy also stated that the woman had traveled throughout the country, and acquired a piece of material from all the then forty-eight states. The names of the states are appliqued by use of lazy daisy and French knot embroidery stitching. It measures 107" x 80".

NINE-PATCH QUILT AND
THE QUILT PROTECTOR

When we were gathering together quilts at the Museum of Appalachia to be photographed, we found this one in an old quilt chest in the General Bunch Cabin. I remembered vividly when I bought this pine quilt chest, thirty years previously.

It sat on the front porch of the old log house where Kellie and Rufus Eledge lived in a narrow hollow in the Smoky Mountain section of Sevier County, Tennessee. Singer Dolly Parton and her family were their neighbors.

The squares in the nine-patch blocks are made of striped, hand-spun, and hand-woven material. I feel sure that this fabric was made in the loom house located a few feet from the Eledge cabin. I bought numerous blankets, coverlets, and garments made of striped material similar to that found in the quilt. My assumption is that the quilt top was made from scraps of old dresses and petticoats.

The other interesting and unusual feature about this quilt is the ten-inch wide protective covering which is fitted over one end of it on the right side as it is shown in the photograph. Although it appears not to have been a widespread addition, it is a most practical innovation. When the protective piece became soiled by dirty little fingers tucking it underneath the chins of small children, or from grandpa's chin whiskers, then it could be removed easily, washed and replaced, thereby eliminating the need to launder the entire quilt. This covering is made of cotton and has been basted to the quilt.

This is the only quilt I have found with such a covering, and I have talked with only two people who were familar with the practice. One was Mildred Locke, the well known quilter from Bell Buckle who is discussed extensively in Chapter VIII, and the other is Margaret Heaton, a native of Kansas. Margaret remembers both her mother and her grandmother using such strips to protect the quilts and also to protect chins from the rough textured, heavy woolen quilts.

LAWRENCE STOOKSBURY'S
CHILDHOOD CRAZY QUILT

In 1896, when Lawrence Stooksbury was about 5 years old, the youngest of fourteen children, his sister Pearl supervised the making of this family Crazy quilt for him. The other

sisters each made a block and signed their names: Hattie; Nola; Lillie; Nannie; and Ethel. They decorated it throughout with floral designs, and they added the phrases, "Home Sweet Home," "Gone Home," the date "1896," indicating the year it was started, and "1900," denoting the year in which it was finished.

The girls had young Lawrence place his hand on one section and they traced around it with a pencil, then embroidered his handprint. Above this they wrote in pencil "Remember," but only the "R" was embroidered. It is not known why this part was left unfinished.

Pearl was always sickly, and when she died of tuberculosis as a young unmarried woman, Lawrence came to treasure the quilt more than ever. He took it and cared for it all his life. His daughter Willie, who now owns the quilt, remembers how carefully her father guarded it through the years.

"He always kept it in a little green trunk, and we children were never allowed to look inside. Sometimes he'd get it out and show it to us, and tell us about how his sisters made it, but even then we were not allowed to touch it. He always thought the world of that quilt — and he saw that it was took care of. On a few very special occasions him and mother would use it as a bed, cover; but very seldom."

Unlike most of the Victorian Crazy quilts, this one is made mostly from woolen scraps. It measures 72" x 64".

MISS TEACHER'S FRIENDSHIP QUILT

A most unusual quilt-making project came about in 1928 when some of Jeanette Norman's eighth grade students decided to make a quilt for her hope chest. Jeanette had only a high school education when she started teaching in the fall of 1927 in the coal mining town of Briceville, Anderson County, Tennessee. Her monthly salary was $55.

Jeanette served as a substitute teacher at Lake City Elementary School. There were twenty-six teachers in the school and anytime one of them was absent, she invariably requested that "Miss" Galloway be called as the substitute. She was friendly and vivacious, but in the classroom she was "all business." She once said, "If a teacher has to do more than to gently tap her pencil on the desk to get the student's attention, there is something wrong."

She was strict, but she was loved by her students. Perhaps that's why those young girls in her first class wanted to do something special for her. One might think the idea of making a quilt for the teacher was a ploy on the part of the students to avoid arithmetic and spelling. I asked Jeanette if she allowed the students to work on the quilt during school hours.

Oh, no. We set up a sewing club of the eighth grade and we met every two weeks in some of the homes — mostly in my home. I furnished some of the material, and some of the mothers furnished some of it. Woolen scrape — it's all wool.

There was fourteen in the class — eight girls and six boys. Each girl had a square to make. Of course the boys couldn't sew, but they wanted their names on the quilt; so their sisters or their mothers would work on their squares.

"But the girls did their own sewing?" I asked.
"Yes. Eighth grade girls are quite capable. They could sew, and many of those girls went on to become teachers."

The names of those fourteen children remain sewn in this quilt which was made for "Miss Teacher's" hope chest.

Clint Bailey was the one that started calling me Miss Teacher, and the others soon picked it up. They still call me that — the one's that's living. There's five of the fourteen who are dead, including Clint. You knew him, he drove a school bus for you.

Well, I married that feller (she pointed to her bedridden husband) William Galloway on October 12, 1930. And on our Golden wedding anniversary, I gave this quilt to Clint's two granddaughters. I always thought so much of him, and I knew the granddaughters too. So I gave it to them to keep as a sort of remembrance of their grandfather.

(Photograph by the author)

THE JAMES PETER FRENCH
FRIENDSHIP QUILT
(First Place Winner)

In the fall of 1884, a group of young ladies in Salem Valley, in south Knox County, Tennessee, joined together to make a Friendship Quilt for James Peter French. He was the youngest of the thirteen children of Peter and Malinda Allison French who had settled Salem Valley in 1812. In his mid-thirties at the time, James was said to have known the Bible by heart, and was an advanced craftsman, farmer, and musical instrument maker. From a prominent and respected family, he must have been one of the community's most eligible bachelors.

As the girls spent many hours quilting together that fall, they wondered aloud who the lucky girl was who was destined to sleep under the quilt they were laboring over. The suspense ended the following April (1885) when James Peter French married Millie Johnson, one of the girls who had prepared a square and whose initials appeared thereon.

The quilt is now in the possession of Mrs. David (Geneva) Jennings of Powell, Tennessee. She is the daughter of Cora French Blazier who was the daughter of James Peter and Millie French. Geneva, who is a librarian with the Knox County school system, entered her grandparents' quilt in the Museum of Appalachia Spring Quilt Show in 1983 and won first place in the category "Quilts With the Most Interesting History."

SARAH ALDRIDGE'S
TENNESSEE WILDFLOWER
(With Alabama Roots)

It was more than appropriate that Sarah Aldridge would choose to quilt the Tennessee Wildflower pattern. She is an accredited flower show judge, has her own wildflower garden, and has intimate knowledge of wildflowers. Even so, when she started to embroider these flowers, she took her threads to her wildflower garden in an endeavor to select just the right hue of thread for each flower.

This quilt, which has the Feathered Wreath design quilted into the solid blocks, won second place in the mixed technique category at the Museum of Appalachia Quilt Show in March 1983.

Sarah moved from Alabama as a girl to Oak Ridge, Tennessee in 1943, only a few months after that overnight atomic city was founded. She has been quilting for only a few years, and I was curious as to what prompted her, a forty-year resident of a modern city, to take up quilting. At first I did not get very definite answers. Then I asked about her mother in Lawrence County, Alabama, and the response to this question was more revealing:

My father died and left my mother with nine children, whose ages ranged from 16 months to 16 years. That was in the Depression and even well established families were going broke every day. But my mother was a good manager and she paid her taxes and her farm payments to the Federal Land Grant Association first, whether there was any money left over or not. We raised cotton mostly, and it was handpicked. We all worked hard and mother managed well and she came out of the Depression with nine grown children and more property than when my father died.

In the winter is when my mother did her quilting. She had a brother-in-law who had a dry cleaning establishment, and he would give her the unclaimed clothes, and she would make them into everyday quilts. She went around the community helping to teach other women how to sew and make quilts.

MOSSIE SHARP BEELER, 96,
AND HER SLAVE QUILT
("Mother" to thirty-six children)

Big Valley is one of the most beautiful valleys in East Tennessee and was among the first to be settled. Starting in 1784, the Sharp family settled there in what is now Union County, an hour's drive north of Knoxville.

There were few slaves in this area, and during the Civil War almost all the people were either neutral or sympathetic to the North. But some of the larger landholders had a few household slaves, and the Sharp family, including Fletcher and Maverna Sharp, were among this group.

They lived in a large white-columned brick home, a mansion by Tennessee standards. One of their household slaves was a young black girl named Rachel Sharp who was set free, probably as a result of Lincoln's Emancipation Proclamation, on January 1, 1863.

Like many former slaves in that section of the valley known as Sharp's Chapel, Rachel continued to live on the old Sharp place after she was freed. She married Tom Palmer and made this quilt for Sarah (Sack) Sharp, the mother of Mossie and the daughter of her former owner. Sack used the quilt a good bit, Mossie recalled, and upon her death in 1935, it fell to Mossie, who has cared for it ever since.

Mossie was born in 1887. She early became a self-reliant woman and learned the art of farming and cattle raising. She helped embalm the dead, deliver babies, and she learned to make quilts. "Oh, I've made a many a quilt," she said.

During this time, according to her son Woody, she raised thirty-three boys, and three girls. These she brought to her home from a Knoxville institute for homeless and orphaned children. Of those thirty-six, she adopted one — whose name was Woody Williamson. I've bought old relics and antiques from Mossie for many years and found her to be a most shrewd and able trader. As Woody says, "She can trade with the best of them." She had a large farm, worked hard, managed well, was extremely thrifty, and eventually sold her chattels and hundreds of acres and retired to her orange groves near Ochee, Florida. When she learned of the Quilt Show at the Museum of Appalachia in March of 1983, she had Woody call and tell me that she was coming. Indeed she did. She traveled several hundred miles, confined to a wheelchair, with her treasured quilt in her lap.

The quilt, according to Mossie, was made form cotton and tow, which is a form of flax — hence linen. It is stuffed with cotton. The appliqued pattern is unknown to the author.

HOMER SLIGER'S
WORLD WAR II QUILT

Every day the fear of opening her mail box became greater for Betty Sliger during the World War II years. She had two sons fighting in the Pacific, and news came often in the community about a neighbor boy who was killed or missing in action.

One can hardly imagine the anguish and the helplessness that Betty and a million other mothers felt. As the war wore on the utter frustration became worse. What could she do, other than to write every day — and pray?

Well, Betty found something else to do. She decided to make a quilt for each of her soldier sons. By so doing she somehow felt close to them, and the attentiveness and detailed planning required in designing and making these quilts helped to alleviate her worry.

One of the quilts was made for her son Arrants, and the one shown here was made for her son Homer Sliger, who now lives in Sweetwater, Tennessee. It was given to him by his joyous mother when he returned unharmed from the Philippines, after the war ended. Betty died in 1974, and Homer treasures the quilt even more now.

D.A.R. regent of 1980-1983, Mrs. James Harrison. The Pledge:

> Three white stars on a field of blue,
> God keep them strong and ever true,
> It is with pride and love that we,
> Salute the flag of Tennessee.

The quilt, 82" x 109" took nine months to make and required approximately 550 man (woman) hours. The quilting was done by the ladies in Gibbs community in Northeast Knox County. It was presented to Mrs. James Harrison at the George Washington luncheon in Knoxville on February 19th, 1983, in appreciation of her 3 years service as Tennessee's state regent of the Daughters of the American Revolution.

Pictured on the left side of the quilt are: Emma Dunn seated nearest the quilt; seated beside her, Edna Monroe; standing at left, Frances Torbett; standing left center, Lucy Steele Harrison to whom the quilt was presented; and standing in the rear at left is Mary Underwood.

On the right side of the quilt are: Alma Daugherty seated nearest the quilt; Alice Buford seated to the right; Alma Blankenship standing at front right; Kathleen Portwood, right center standing; and Elise Jenkins right rear.

URN OF FLOWERS

At a recent antique show and sale in Nashville, we marveled at the number and quality of quilts; and at the prices they commanded. This Urn of Flowers quilt shown here is a good example, priced at $9,500.00. It is believed to have been made in Maryland, and is dated 1850 in the quilting, and measures 81" x 88". (Photograph courtesy Thomas K. Woodard, New York City.)

DR. ROBERT HARVEY'S PRIZE WINNING QUILT

One of the eye-catchers at the 1983 Annual Senior Citizens Quilt Show in Erwin, Tennessee was a quilt made and entered by Dr. Robert E. Harvey. It had been awarded first place in its category.

Even though I was much impressed by the beauty of the quilt itself. I was equally interested in the person who made it inasmuch as he was a man, as well as a physician. This was an unusual combination, I thought, for a quilter. In response to my letter to him, Dr. Harvey offered the following explanation.

I never did any quilting until about six months after my retirement on July 1, 1979. A friend was with me when I asked a clerk at a craft shop about a small cross stitch piece to see if I could do it. She did not have any small items but a full size "Quilt Top." I laughed about this but my friend bought it and gave it to me as a Christmas present.

I started working on it in January, 1980 and had it finished by April 1, 1980. One of the girls at the Senior Citizens had been my office nurse for ten years and she insisted on me entering the show. I did not have patience enough to quilt it or any of them, so the ex-nurse got one of her Senior Citizens to quilt my top. It won three Blue Ribbons, including Best of Show, Peoples Choice, and Men's Division. So I decided to do more quilt tops, along with table cloths and pillow cases.

I am 72 years old, have practiced (General Practice) in Erwin, Tennessee since 1937 except for 5 1/2 years duty in World War II. As for therapeutic

evaluation, its just a good and rewarding way to spend spare time with "good" results. I am finishing my 6th quilt top at the present.

JULIA NEEDHAM, NATIONAL PRIZE WINNING QUILTER

Julia Overton Needham recalls that when she was 5 years old, living in Knoxville, Tennessee, her mother started to quilt during the revival of interest in quilting in those Depression years. She remembers punching the needle through the quilt and then having to crawl under the quilting frame to push it back. Like most quilters, Julia is exuberant when talking about her quilting. She puts it most succinctly when she says, "It just consumes you."

Julia used this old pattern, Blazing Star, but set the stars inside squares created by the incorporation of what she calls Streaks of Lightning. "I worked on this quilt for six or seven months," Julia admits. "I worked some every day. Some days I worked a lot longer than others, but I worked some every day — didn't feel right if I didn't do something on it each day."

It won "Best of Show" in the annual Smoky Mountain Quilt Competition in Oak Ridge in 1982, and it took first place in the "hand pieced and hand quilted" category in the Tennessee Valley Agriculture and Industry Fair in Knoxville. It won first place in the same category at another quilt show in Parson, Tennessee.

I never had a lesson on quilting. My mother quilted a little but it was just a flash in the pan with her. She wasn't in good health, and she never quilted much. But I was just excited to death with sewing and quilting ever since I can remember.

When I was 13 or 14, I made this quilt that I'm holding in the picture — Trip Around the World. I set out in our front yard on Chapman Highway one summer under the shade tree and watched them make it (the highway) into four lanes. That's when I quilted my first quilt by myself. Made it out of dress scraps.

I went to see the Stearns and Foster Collection in Cincinnati in 1977, and that really fired me up. I really got inspired seeing all them beautiful quilts there, and I come home and really started in earnest. Then I entered some quilts in the Smoky Mountain Quilt Show in Oak Ridge, and they really helped and encouraged me. I had just always quilted on my own and never showed my quilts; so those women there were so encouraging, and helpful and that gave me another big push and when I won Best of Show there, of course, that just excited me to death. I keep a quilt up just about all the time. I'm lost if I don't have a quilt set up to work on.

THE BELL TELEPHONE QUILT

As a child, Lola Shelby Sweat often watched her mother make quilts at their home in the Alder Springs section of Campbell County, Tennessee. Although Lola learned to sew, she didn't take up quilting until many years later One day while working at the Bell Telephone Company in Lafollette, she noticed a door mat with the Bell emblem, and the thought immediately struck her: "Why doesn't some-body make a quilt using the telephone in it? Then I said, 'I'll make it myself.' "

And so the Bell Telephone Quilt was conceived. Lola made the quilt and a pillow to match. The pillow won first place in its category in the 1983 Smoky Mountain Quilt Show in Oak Ridge, and the quilt won second place in its category.

When I called Lola regarding the unusual quilt, she informed me that she had just completed her last day with the Bell Telephone Company after thirty years, one month, and a day. (Photograph by the author)

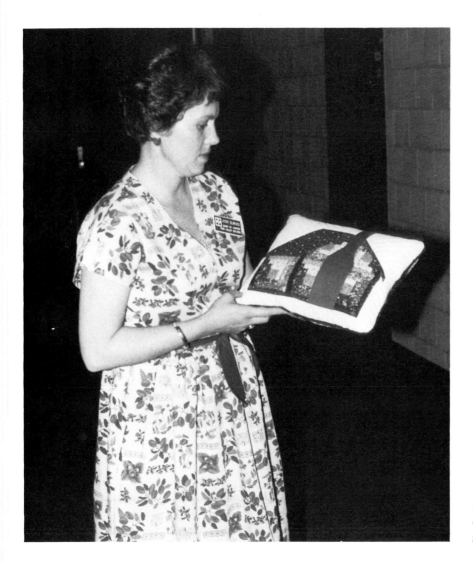

Judy Elwood is shown here during the 1983 Smoky Mountain Quilt Show in Oak Ridge with one of the many pillows entered with a quilt square covering.

FOUR AND TWENTY BLACKBIRDS

Jean Lester grew up in the atomic city of Oak Ridge, Tennessee, married a Knoxville physician, and is the mother of five young children. I was curious about what sparked her interest in quilting, which she started in 1975. "I wanted something to leave for the grandchildren I hope to have someday — something that I myself had made and created."

My curiosity remained as to why she chose quilts for her grandchildren over a thousand other items. I asked about her early childhood, whether she had been exposed in those formative years to sewing and/or quilting. She told me of her childhood years on the plains of eastern Colorado. Her family had come to that wheat growing region directly from the German section of Switzerland and were prodigious seamstresses. "All my clothes were hand-made back then," Jean recalls.

She chose the Four and Twenty Blackbirds idea because she wanted excitement and movement, but it was her husband, Dr. Tom Lester, who actually drew the design which she quilted. It won first place in the category "hand-appliqued, hand-quilted Crib Quilt," in the 1983 Smoky Mountain Quilt Competition and Show. (Photograph by the author)

MILDRED LOCKE, THE QUILTERS' QUILTER

In my contacts with numerous young quilters, the name Mildred Locke kept turning up. As a matter of fact, several very fine quilters, sponsors of quilt shows and exhibits, gave credit to Mildred Locke for their interest in quilts. Many of those people concluded our discussions by saying "You ought to talk with Mildred Locke down at Bell Buckle, Tennessee." When I discovered that the National Quilt Show was being held at Bell Buckle because of Mildred, I made it a point to visit her.

Bell Buckle, located in the very heart of the area which spawned the world famous Tennessee Walking Horses, is located in Middle Tennessee about sixty-five miles southeast of Nashville. It was named, so Mildred has always been told, after a cow bell and a buckle (for holding the leather strap and the bell on the cow's neck) which was found carved on a tree in that area. Ostensibly this carving was placed there by a scout to indicate the site for a group of settlers to stop and graze their livestock.

Mildred and her husband have built a small building at their back door for her quilt shop, and here she has a wide assortment of quilting material and supplies as well as new and used quilts. Inside their home, everything says "quilts." There were quilts on all the beds as spreads, and there were quilts hanging on the walls, on the chairs and couches, as table cloths, and even one hanging as a shower curtain. Mildred advocates *using* quilts as opposed to keeping them stored in climate-controlled areas never, or seldom, seen. She loves them, cares for them carefully and even, I think, talks to them. That is why she wants them with her wherever she is.

Q. Mildred, the obvious question would be how you became interested in quilts and quilting. So many people across the state indicated that they were influenced by you. To what do you attribute your interest? Does it go back to your childhood?

A. Yes. It goes back that far. I love the quilts, I love the patterns, I love the designs, but we had what was called "country quilts." I can remember folding the Sears and Roebuck catalog for my mother to make squares. She'd make the top and she'd put it in the frame and my aunts would come and they would quilt. And they could make a quilt in a day, because they did it in the fan and they did it fast, and it didn't take long. But that quilt was to keep us warm.

I didn't like those quilts. I liked the fancy quilts that had the beautiful feathered designs quilted on them and those that had the beautiful applique, the ones we always kept for company. We didn't ever get to use those things. I was the one that went into the front bedroom and would trace that pattern with my finger, you know, and that's what I wanted to do — I wanted to make quilts like that. I didn't make quilts until we moved back here in 1960. But in the back of my mind, that longing was always there.

Q. You indicated that your aunts would come in to quilt.

A. Yes, it was a quilting bee. They would come and would quilt all day long. It would be my mother, her sister, and her sister-in-law. There were about five of them would quilt together. This was mainly during the winter.

When I was 12 or so, I made me a navy blue shirt, and I was going to work my buttonholes with white thread. Well, I sat right beside Grandmaw, and every white thread had to be exactly the same length, you know. That buttonhole was perfect when I got through. I worked about seven down the front of that shirt. And from then on I thought, 'I won't let Grandmaw see me do anything!' I remember that more than anything, if you're going to do it, do it right.

Q. And that was your father's mother?

A. Yes, she was a perfectionist, and she saw to it that I did it perfect also. I always had sewn — since I was 6 years old or so. My mother always let me use her sewing machine, and I appreciate that too, that she let me do it. I did what I wanted to, and I sewed. When I was a little girl, 7 or 8, and had a dime and went to town, I would buy these dresser sets to embroider, you know, instead of a toy, because that's what I wanted to do. I wanted to do needle work. I've done every kind of needle work, but when we moved back here in 1960, to stay and take care of my mother, you know, I thought to myself, 'I can quilt now — I have the time.' So that's when I started quilting. I started *trying* to quilt let us say. The first I did was a cross-stitch quilt — blue cross-stitch quilt. I didn't know how to quilt. I'd seen my mother do it you know, and the cross-stitch quilt had all these dots on there. I remember when I took it out of the package — I'd ordered it as a kit — and I said 'Hum.' I knew I was going to do all the little X's, but I said, 'If you think I'm gonna put a needle in all those little dots all over this quilt — you're mistaken!' That's what I told the quilt. But after I got it cross-stitched, then I wanted to quilt it. And so, I borrowed some quilting frames — but Edgar doesn't like for me to borrow anything, he likes for me to have my own. So, he went to a sale and he bought me some old-fashioned quilting frames.

Well, the only place I could put them up was upstairs. So we put them up in the north room upstairs, and I would go up there and I would quilt. I knew I was not doing what I should do. I was not doing the right thing. It didn't look right and I couldn't decide if you made your thread to go from this dot to that dot, or whether you went through the middle or what. All during that quilt, I did all sorts of different kinds of work trying to do what I knew should be done. But I never was satisfied with what I did on that quilt. I finished it and bound it, and started another one.

Q. Was this the first one you made on your own?

A. Yes. But the quilting designs on the kits are gorgeous, you know, they have those Feather Wreaths — and that's what got me hooked. As soon as I'd quilted one Feather Wreath, I knew I was going to quilt a lot of those you know, because they're real, real pretty. But my quiltin' didn't look right. So, I was sitting in there on the couch quilting a pillow cushion on a little quilt-as-you-go frame, and this lady from Bell Buckle came out, her name is Bess Arnold. She came out and she says, 'Mildred, you're not doing that right.' She took that needle and she sat the thimble back at the back of that needle and she started this little stitch just like that. That was just like an electric light came on — I knew *THAT* was the way Momma and my aunts had quilted all that time! When I teach it, they have to teach their fingers to do that. But I didn't have to learn it like that, because I'd been searching for it. I was so excited! My husband was working then — he'd come home at midnight. Well, I was still quilting at midnight, but I didn't even go to bed then — I just kept on quilting because I had found what I wanted to know.

Q. I'm not sure I understand that technique.

A. I know. It's something you have to be shown. See, what I did to that first quilt was I sewed it together. I sewed my three layers together. But quilting is a stitch — you were talking about the three dimensional look — it gives you that three dimensional look. A lot of women are sewing instead of quilting; and there's a big difference.

Now Miss Clemmie Simmons in Shelbyville gave me a lot of hints about quilting. I'd go to her and I'd talk to her, you know, and she'd show me things and gave me a lot of hints about it. I read every book I could get, too, but books...people think if it's written in a book — it's right. But that's not true. I bought this book written by a lady in Alabama, and I had done everything that it said to do to make a Log Cabin block. And I couldn't come out with this block. I told Edgar, I said, 'We are going to Lineville, Alabama.' When I say we're going somewhere he says O.K., you know, so we went to Lineville, Alabama, to see this lady who had made this Log Cabin block — quilt-as-you-go pattern in this book. I went to see her and I said to her, 'I have done step by step, over and over, exactly what you say to do. When I get through, this is not on this block exactly right.' She said, 'Oh, you just cut that background block just a little larger then you trim it off when you get through.' So I knew then that you use your common sense.

Q. Mildred, I think we were trying to determine how you became such a national influence on quilting, and we started out with your mother and your aunts that would come in and help quilt, etc. What happened after you made the first one and how did you get into the buisness?

A. Well, after I made that cross-stitch quilt — then I wanted to make a pieced quilt. I had always wanted to make a Lone Star, so I made a yellow Lone Star. Yellow and brown Lone Star. I made a lot of quilts. Then my son got ready to get married and I made him a quilt. I was making quilts and I was enjoying quilts and I was having a good time. Then it got to where other people were interested in quilts.

Q. Were you selling some of yours?

A. No, no I wasn't selling any at all. When I finally started selling quilts, a friend of mine called me and asked me to go on the tour of homes at the pilgrimage in Natchez, Mississippi. Well, by then — well, my mother lived until 1964, and my father lived until '71, and all the time in there I was just making things for us. It was after this that

Source Books

Bacon, Lenice Ingram. *American Patchwork Quilts*. New York: Bonanza, 1973.

Bannister, Barbara; Ford, Edna Paris. *State Capitals Quilt Blocks*. New York: Dover, 1977.

Bishop, Robert. *New Discoveries in American Quilts*. New York: E.P. Dutton Company, 1975.

Bishop, Robert. *Quilts, Coverlets, Rugs and Samplers*. New York: Alfred A. Knopf, 1982.

Bishop, Robert; Safanda, Elizabeth. *A Gallery of Amish Quilts*. New York: E.P. Dutton Company, 1976.

Cooper, Patricia; Buferd, Norma Bradley. *The Quilters; Women and Domestic Art, An Oral History*. New York: Anchor Press/Doubleday, 1977.

Edwards, Phoebe. *Anyone Can Quilt*. New York: The Benjamin Company, 1975.

Elwood, Judy; Tennery, Joyce; Richardson, Alice. *Tennessee Quilting; Designs Plus Patterns*, 1982.

Hall, Carrie A.; Kretsinger, Rose G. *The Romance of the Patchwork Quilt in America*. New York: Bonanza Books.

Hinson, Dolores A. *Quilting Manual*. New York: Dover, 1966.

Holland, Nina. *Pictorial Quilting*. South Brunswick and New York: A.S. Barnes and Company. London: Thomas Yoseloff Limited, 1978.

Holstein, Jonathan; Finley, John. *Kentucky Quilts 1800 - 1900*. Louisville: The Kentucky Quilt Project, Incorporated, 1982.

Houck, Carter; Miller, Myron. *American Quilts And How to Make Them*. New York: Charles Scribner's Sons, 1975.

Ickis, Marguerite. *The Standard Book of Quilt Making and Collecting*. New York: Dover, 1949.

James, Michael. *The Second Quiltmaker's Handbook; Creative Approaches to Contemporary Quilt Design*. Englewood Cliffs, New Jersey: Prentiss - Hall, 1981.

Khin, Yvonne M. *The Collectors Dictionary of Quilt Names & Patterns*. Washington, D.C.: Acropolis, 1980.

Layton, Miriam; Walker, Patricia A.; Williams, Marian. *The I'd-Rather-Be-Quilting Cookbook*. Seattle: Madrona, 1982.

Leman, Bonnie; Martin, Judy. *Log Cabin Quilts*. Denver: Moon Over the Mountain, 1980.

Marshall, Martha. *Many Patches Ago; The Story of Quilting Within the Mountain Region*. Rogersville, Tennessee: East Tennessee Printing, 1981.

McKim, Ruby Short. *One Hundred and One Patchwork Patterns*. New York: Dover, 1962.

Mills, Susan Winter. *American Quilt Patterns*. New York: Arco, 1980.

Montgomery, Eric. *How It All Began, The Ulster-American Folk Park*. Camphill, Company Tyrone, Northern Ireland: Scotch-Irish Trust of Ulster, 1982.

Pforr, Effie Chalmers. *Award Winning Quilts*. Birmingham: Oxmoor House, 1974.

Stafford, Carleton L.; Bishop, Robert. *Americas Quilts and Coverlets*. New York: Weathervane, 1974.

Index

F

G

H

N

O

P

Q

R

S

T

U

V

W

Y